PRAISE FOR *PRACTICAL LEADERSHIP IN COMMUNITY COLLEGES*

"For both current and aspiring leaders, *Practical Leadership in Community Colleges* offers a highly effective balance of historical, contextual, and practical information. Grounded in clear-cut fundamentals of mission management, the book adds insightful questions for each chapter that will help individuals and leadership teams frame key issues in such critical areas as accountability, diversity and inclusion, finance, and campus security. In the face of the rising leadership turnover at community colleges and the increasing complexity of the leadership role, the book will help prepare campuses for what many foresee as perpetual and often dramatic change."

—**Walter G. Bumphus,** president and CEO,
American Association of Community Colleges

"With an emphasis on the practical, Boggs and McPhail take on such difficult issues as 'success' versus quality, the rising cost of a college education, the 'completion agenda,' declining state support, and more. This book serves as a field guide for current presidents already immersed in the fray, as well as a primer and reality check for anyone who aspires to become a community college president. For both groups it is a must-read."

—**Rob Jenkins,** "Two-Year Track" columnist for
The Chronicle of Higher Education; author of *Building a Career in America's
Community Colleges*

"As George Boggs and Christine McPhail point out in this important book, American community colleges are on the brink of massive changes nationwide. I found this book to be useful and inspiring. The authors' balanced approach to presenting existing challenges and opportunities for the next generation of colleges and their leaders is refreshing. The authors make the clear and convincing case that a bold commitment to reinvention along with the skillful management of issues of diversity, inclusion, and equity are key to riding the wave of change to new and exciting shores."

—**Eduardo J. Padrón,** president, Miami Dade College

"This is a 'must read' for community college leaders everywhere. Written by two national leaders with more than seventy years of leadership experience and success in community colleges, the book addresses the issues and challenges facing today's and tomorrow's community colleges. I expect to see the book utilized in graduate classes and in leadership development workshops on campuses everywhere."

—**John E. Roueche,** president, Roueche Graduate Center,
National American University

"Every few years a breath of fresh air blows through the halls of academe bringing fresh insights and creative perspectives for those of us who have been suffocating from pat answers and stale platitudes. *Practical Leadership in Community Colleges* by two seasoned thought leaders, George Boggs and Christine McPhail, is a testament to enlightened common sense for community college leaders. This book is a rare combination of scholarly work and practical advice. It will become the key go-to resource for every leader who wants to survive and prevail in the community college world."

—**Terry O'Banion,** chair of the graduate faculty, National American University, and president emeritus, League for Innovation in the Community College

"Authors George Boggs and Christine McPhail team up to provide a thoughtful, relevant, essential and urgent insight into contemporary and emerging challenges facing community college leaders. The timeliness of this text cannot be understated given the unrelenting nature of change, combined with the seemingly rapid acceleration and diversity of heretofore uncommon issues facing higher education. This book is a vital must-read for all community college leaders, aspiring leaders, and boards of trustees. I am grateful to these well-known, national leaders for advancing this discussion."

—**Daniel J. Phelan,** president and CEO,
Jackson College

"Leading our nation's community colleges is perhaps now more difficult than ever before, which is why *Practical Leadership in Community Colleges* could not come at a more opportune time. We can't lead with outdated theories; we need nimble, nuanced thinking and creative innovation, which the authors set the stage for in this volume. I highly recommend the book. It finely balances the best of theory with the most recent in practical issues our current and future leaders need to consider. Well done!"

—**Rufus Glasper,** chancellor, Maricopa Community Colleges

"In this new resource, George Boggs and Christine McPhail tell the story of the history and role of community colleges and relate the current pressures and challenges confronting all of higher education to this very special sector of the education system. Their work is an essential guide for community college leadership—presidents, senior administrators, faculty and the governing boards that hold the fiduciary authority to advance the changes needed throughout the system. I urge board members to take a look at the messages in this new contribution."

—**Richard Legon,** president, Association of Governing
Boards of Universities and Colleges (AGB)

PRACTICAL LEADERSHIP IN COMMUNITY COLLEGES

Navigating Today's Challenges

PRACTICAL LEADERSHIP IN COMMUNITY COLLEGES

Navigating Today's Challenges

George R. Boggs
Christine J. McPhail

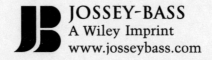

JOSSEY-BASS
A Wiley Imprint
www.josseybass.com

Library of Congress Cataloging-in-Publication Data

Names: Boggs, George R., author. | McPhail, Christine Johnson, author.
Title: Practical leadership in community colleges : navigating today's challenges / George R. Boggs, Christine J. McPhail.
Description: Hoboken, New Jersey : John Wiley & Sons, 2016. | Includes bibliographical references and index.
Identifiers: LCCN 2016006355 | ISBN 9781119095156 (cloth) ISBN 9781119095149 (ePDF) | ISBN 9781119094883 (epub)
Subjects: LCSH: Community colleges—United States—Administration. | Educational leadership—United States.
Classification: LCC LB2341 .B553 2016 | DDC 378.1/5430973—dc23 LC record available at http://lccn.loc.gov/2016006355

Cover design: Wiley
Cover image: © epicurean/Getty Images, Inc.

Printed in the United States of America

FIRST EDITION

HB Printing   10 9 8 7 6 5 4 3 2 1

CONTENTS

FOREWORD

Dr. Belle Wheelan
President, Southern Association of Colleges and Schools,
Commission on Colleges

There is much truth to the adage, "Experience is the best teacher," and the authors of this book have much experience to share in the field of community college leadership. Higher education, specifically in the community college sector, has undergone a major transition over the past decade with the development of and emphasis on workforce training programs, including such innovations as Massive Open Online Courses (MOOCs), badges as symbols of achievement, and Competency Based Education (CBE) Programs. There are many who feel that this emphasis threatens the very fiber of institutions that have a traditional liberal arts focus. Because community colleges have always had workforce development as a part of their mission, they have continued to provide just-in-time responses to them all.

In order for institutions of higher education to remain current and respond effectively to these changes, institutional leaders must also remain current in a myriad of areas. Some of these areas are common to all segments of higher education and include such things as financing and legal issues, personnel issues, and governance. Although curricular issues are probably the ones that will demand the most "new thinking" within community colleges, there are others, including the changing mission of what we know today as community colleges, that demand institutions to rethink how they do business or run the risk of becoming obsolete. The shift from student access to student success, the provision of upper-division programs (baccalaureate), and the financing of public institutions will all demand a new way of thinking specifically for community colleges. It is on these shifts that this book focuses.

If one were to believe all of the crises about higher education that have been written in the higher education "rags," then no one would ever want to take on a leadership role in any institution of higher education today.

It wouldn't take much for even the strongest and most effective leader to become discouraged from moving into a top leadership position when the pressures and changes are presented; however, the rewards of leadership are many, and preparation in meeting them will be paramount. The ability to improve the effectiveness of an institution, to positively affect the lives of the students who matriculate there and the communities in which they live, and the ability to motivate faculty and staff to improve student success through innovation and creativity are still the successes which drive effective leaders. This book provides road markers for those who choose to travel the road to leadership in community colleges.

During their forty-plus year careers, these authors have provided leadership in several community colleges, as well as at the national level. Their experiences have led them to work with both seasoned and budding leaders to ensure their preparation for the challenges that face them currently and will face them in the future. They have witnessed the metamorphosis of community colleges during nearly half a century and weathered many a storm involving governance systems, faculty unions, downturns in the economy, and even uproars in the community in order to move institutions forward. The lessons they have learned comprise a significant part of this book and will serve future leaders well in gaining insight to steer their new ways of thinking and provide effective leadership.

Additionally, external groups such as state and federal legislators, business communities, accreditors, and policy groups have begun to weigh in on what institutions of higher education should look like, whom they should serve, and how their students should be served. Demands for more public accountability, transparency and availability of information, and more stringent responses to safety and security needs on campus are being made from every corner. Given the comparison shopper notion of choosing which institution of higher education to attend, the demand for more data has affected every decision educational leaders must now make in order to ensure robust enrollments and quality programs. Learning to use the data effectively is a talent that must be cultivated.

In addition to the traditional planning, budgeting, and financing courses currently included in graduate programs in higher education leadership, these programs must now include courses in "the use of data in making decisions," "how to know if your campus is safe enough," "how to increase the completion rates of students without reducing access or inflating student grades," and "how to assess student learning outcomes" in order to provide adequate responses to the forces colleges face and prepare effective leaders.

From mission and purpose to student success and all of the additional areas that have evolved, leaders who read this book will have a head start in learning how to navigate the waters much more smoothly. Knowing the challenges prior to accepting a position of leadership will better prepare the leaders of the future. Instead of taking a position of leadership and then either burning out or becoming disgruntled, by reading this book potential leaders will be aware of the emerging challenges they will face and be able to effectively confront them head on.

I commend the authors for sharing their expertise and only wish I had had such a reference when I began my career all those years ago.

PREFACE

There are few careers that can compare to those in community colleges. The institutions truly make a difference in the lives of people and in the well-being of communities. The rewards are visible at graduation ceremonies, performances, athletic events, and exhibits, where students—who would not otherwise have had a chance to pursue higher education or vocational training—demonstrate and are recognized for achieving goals they and their families might only have dreamed to accomplish. The benefits provided by the colleges extend to the community by providing trained employees to local businesses and through the economic impact they have. Because of the demographics of their students, community colleges can help to close achievement gaps and keep our nation secure and competitive.

For community colleges to realize their maximum impact, strong, stable, courageous, and effective leadership is essential. Leadership—at all levels of the institution—makes a significant difference in how well the institution serves its students and its communities. However, leadership in community colleges has become increasingly complex. The colleges are being pushed to increase the success rates of their students—including the most at-risk students in higher education—and to close achievement gaps in an environment of declining public support and calls for increased accountability for outcomes. The very mission of the institutions is being changed by both internal and external forces. Governance of the institutions has become more challenging because of both internal strife and external political influence. In the wake of natural disasters and human-made tragedies, college leaders are dealing with increased concerns for campus safety and security and responding to an increase in government mandates and reporting requirements.

The purpose of this book is to assist educators, leaders, and aspiring leaders to anticipate and to manage emerging issues and to assist trustees in their oversight of institutions that are faced with significant challenges. Although the recommendations are based in theory, the focus is on practical responses to issues. The authors hope to encourage discussions of issues at cabinet meetings, in committee and task force meetings, and in leadership development programs so that leaders are better prepared to deal with the leadership issues they will be faced with.

How This Book Is Structured

In chapter 1, we discuss the origin of issues and the importance of anticipating them and of their effective management. A model for issue management is presented.

In chapter 2, we discuss how the community colleges' open-door policies provide access to and opportunity for education through programs and services that serve as the foundation for life-changing perspectives for individuals and responsiveness to community needs. We highlight some of the mission-related issues that community college leaders will have to navigate as they focus on maintaining the open door and responding to student needs, internal and external policies, and mandates.

Contemporary accountability efforts like those we articulate in chapter 3 indicate that community colleges are undergoing major transformation in terms of what it means to be accountable. The discussion in this chapter focuses on the importance of transparency and how today's community college leaders are expected to build environments that demonstrate through quantifiable results how responsive they are to internal and external stakeholders.

The financing of community colleges continues to be a major issue of concern for community college educators. In chapter 4, we discuss a wide range of changes in the community college sector that affect funding for community colleges. Contemporary community college leaders will be expected to manage the institutions in the midst of growing demands from internal and external stakeholders, increased governmental policies and mandates, and shifting relationships with business communities that look to community colleges for the training of skilled workers.

In chapter 5, we discuss how the increasingly diverse student populations have presented new and different leadership challenges for community college educators. Diversity, equity, and inclusion (DEI) issues emerge inside and outside the classroom. The discussion highlights how some of these DEI challenges are influencing and enhancing learning outcomes for underrepresented students, faculty engagement, and overall institutional improvements.

In the community college setting, a variety of groups have a stake in the business of the college. The discussion in chapter 6 demonstrates that governance problems are not always easy for community college leaders to solve and that communications and media relations strategies often determine the seriousness of an issue. Community college leaders must strive to support governance systems that ensure stakeholders have appropriate opportunities to engage in decision making at the institution. We make the point that communication and media relations strategies are important tools for leaders.

In chapter 7, we discuss the importance of community colleges' ability to respond to the changing external and internal environments. We highlight recent changes and point out some factors that may serve as barriers to organizational change. We remind community college leaders that the college's capacity to respond to change is essential for the current and future welfare of the institution.

Chapter 8 deals with safety and security issues. Leaders need to ensure that campus emergency preparedness plans are up to date, employees and students receive necessary training, and mandated reports are filed on time. All too often, college leaders need to respond to problems created by natural disasters, accidents, or violence against students and employees. More recently, leaders are finding they have to respond to concerns about athletic injuries and problems with cybersecurity.

At the end of each chapter, we present issues to consider. Case studies or scenarios are also provided throughout the text. Our hope is that these issues and case studies will inspire in-depth discussions at presidents' and chancellors' cabinet meetings, in committee meetings, and in leadership development classrooms. There are no "cookie cutter" answers for addressing these issues or responding to cases, but thinking deeply about them will prepare leadership teams for the inevitable difficult issues they will face as they lead these dynamic institutions that are so important to our society.

The common thread throughout the discussion in all of the chapters is that the issues community college leaders currently face—and will have to address in the future—will be different and more complex than those faced by community college leaders in the past. However, too many community college leaders tell us they lack the preparation to address these issues in an effective manner. This book provides both incumbent and aspiring leaders with new ideas and proactive approaches to the task of issue management in community colleges. It will help administrators, faculty, and boards of trustees be better prepared to address today's and tomorrow's challenges.

How to Use This Book

Why does a community college educator need a copy of *Practical Leadership in Community Colleges: Navigating Today's Challenges*? For a number of reasons, many leaders may not have time or the desire to think about their own personal growth and renewal—or even the professional development of their leadership teams. We have come to believe that continual personal growth for community college educators is a necessity rather than an option for today or a resolution for the future. This is not necessarily a book designed for reading top to bottom. Rather, it is a resource of timely information that can be used on a continual basis. The issues are all related to challenges that community college leaders have responsibility for addressing at their institutions. It is designed to be a resource tool for community college leaders and prospective leaders to learn how to manage important issues and to help their institutions in the transformation process.

HOW ADMINISTRATORS CAN USE THE BOOK

- Focused discussions (around the issues) with leadership teams
- Grow-Your-Own college leadership institutes or academies
- Simulations and scenario leadership development programs
- Resource and reference tool for project development
- Functional or topical modules (e.g., designed to be inserted into existing college professional growth activities)

HOW FACULTY CAN USE THE BOOK

- Issue discussions and debates with colleagues and/or students
- Contemporary issues papers for professional associations
- Resource and reference tool for classroom discussion

HOW GOVERNING BOARDS CAN USE THE BOOK

- Orientation to the issues confronting community colleges
- Board retreats/leadership summits or workshops
- Functional or topical modules (e.g., designed to be inserted into continuing board training efforts)

HOW LEADERSHIP DEVELOPMENT TRAINERS CAN USE THE BOOK

- Career and executive coaching
- Leadership institutes

○ Focus groups and workshops

○ Stand-alone workshops (e.g., required capstone workshops; voluntary extracurricular workshops)

○ Grow-Your-Own leadership institutes or academies focusing on each topic over an extended period of time

HOW EDUCATIONAL ASSOCIATIONS CAN USE THE BOOK

○ Promote annual training conferences that allow members to work cooperatively with each other to apply solutions to the issues in a professional setting.

○ Offer webinars or other training events addressing selected issues to improve leadership skills.

○ Promote regional "networks" so that individuals and institutions can learn from others who have successfully (or unsuccessfully) confronted the same issues under similar circumstances.

○ Use the suggestions in the book to offer technical assistance to individual and institutional members who may be struggling with the issues in the workplace.

○ Use the issue analysis in the book to advocate for public and private resources to sustain research and technical assistance to develop practitioners who understand higher education issues.

We bring together more than seventy years of higher education experience in higher education to write *Practical Leadership in Community Colleges: Navigating Today's Challenges.* The book is a collection of chapters designed for community college educators, leaders, and policy makers to use as tools to create a framework for managing key issues in community colleges. Readers can open it and find a particular issue that they are facing on any given day. No matter what position the educator holds, the reader will have the necessary information to successfully analyze the issue within the context of the community college setting. From decades of experience in the field, we can say with some authority that people who are proactive in gaining the skills to manage the emerging issues that their institutions face are more effective leaders. They see themselves as inherently powerful and having the ability to control elements of the situations in which they find themselves. We encourage community college leaders to use this book to expand the leadership capacity at their institutions.

ACKNOWLEDGMENTS

The authors thank their spouses, Ann Boggs and Dr. Irving Pressley McPhail, for their support and understanding, the colleagues who have served with them and helped them to understand how important leadership really is, and their students from whom they learn every day.

We greatly appreciate those colleagues who took their valuable time to review our text and to provide comments. They motivate us to do the best work we can.

We also thank the leaders of America's community colleges for their commitment to close achievement gaps and to improve the lives of people in communities across America. Community college educators and leaders serve the most at-risk students and receive the lowest percentage of public resources. They are responsible for navigating today's challenges, and we hope our work will assist them to succeed.

ABOUT THE AUTHORS

George R. Boggs is president and CEO emeritus of the American Association of Community Colleges (AACC) and superintendent/president emeritus of Palomar College in San Marcos, California. He continues to be an active consultant, teacher, author, and speaker. Dr. Boggs has published more than a hundred articles, books, and chapters on areas related to higher education. He is a professor in the community college doctoral programs at San Diego State University and National American University.

Dr. Boggs holds a bachelor's degree in chemistry from The Ohio State University, a master's degree in chemistry from the University of California at Santa Barbara, and a PhD in educational administration from The University of Texas at Austin.

He serves as a member of the National Academy of Sciences Board on Science Education and on the Phi Theta Kappa International Student Honor Society Board, serving as chair. Dr. Boggs chaired the Organizing Committee for the December 2011 STEM Summit sponsored by the National Academy of Sciences. He is a past chair of the Board of the World Federation of Colleges and Polytechnics and consults internationally. During his career, Dr. Boggs has served on many boards, commissions, and committees, including those of the American Council on Education, the Education Testing Service (ETS), the National Center for Postsecondary Research, the National Center for Community College Student Engagement, the National Science Foundation (NSF), the National Science Board's Commission on 21st Century STEM Education, the Western Association of Schools and Colleges (WASC), the Accrediting Board for Engineering and Technology (ABET), the Community College League of California, the Washington Higher Education Secretariat, and the American Association of Community Colleges, serving as board chair in 1993–94.

Dr. Boggs has been recognized by the Public Broadcasting System with its Terry O'Banion Prize for Teaching and Learning for "triggering the most significant educational movement of the past decade." He is a Distinguished Graduate of The University of Texas. Dr. Boggs has been recognized by the Chair Academy, the National Institute for Staff and

Organizational Development (NISOD), the Association of California Community College Administrators, the Association of Community College Trustees, the American Association of Community Colleges, the Society for College and University Planning, the National Council on Marketing and Public Relations, NASPA Student Affairs Administrators, the San Marcos Chamber of Commerce, the City of Vista, and the US Congress. Dr. Boggs is listed in *Who's Who in America* and six other *Who's Who* directories.

Christine Johnson McPhail is emerita professor of higher education and founder of the Community College Leadership Doctoral Program at Morgan State University and president emerita of Cypress College in Cypress, California. She currently serves as the managing principal for the McPhail Group LLC, a higher education consulting firm, and as a leadership coach for Achieving the Dream, a national reform network that helps more community college students succeed.

Dr. McPhail holds an associate of arts degree from Fresno City College, a bachelor's degree in social work from California State University, Fresno, a master's degree in higher education counseling from California State University, Fresno, and an EdD in higher education from the University of Southern California. Dr. McPhail has served as a national advisor for the Gates Foundation's Completion by Design, the Community College Survey of Student Engagement (CCSSE), and the National Center for Postsecondary Research (NCPR) at the Community College Research Center (CCRC). She is a past member of the boards of directors for the American Association of Community Colleges (AACC) and the Council for the Study of Community Colleges (CSCC). Dr. McPhail has also served as the affirmative action officer, Division J, American Education Research Association (AERA), and on the editorial board for the *Community College Journal of Research and Practice*. She has published numerous articles and book chapters and books on topics pertaining to higher education.

Dr. McPhail's work has been recognized by local state and national associations. She was the recipient of the AACC National Leadership Award, the 2008 League of Innovation's Terry O'Banion Leadership Award, the State of Maryland Governor's Citation, the Citizen Citation from the City of Baltimore, the Maryland Women for Responsible Government Leadership Award, and the National Council of Black American Affairs' Pioneer Award for promoting equity in higher education. The Community College League of California; California State University, Fresno; and Fresno City College have recognized her as a distinguished alumna. She was also inducted into the State Center Community College's Hall of Fame.

Dr. McPhail is the editor for one of AACC's best-selling publications, *Establishing and Sustaining Learning Centered Community Colleges.* She was the featured international keynote speaker at the Guardian Further Education and Skills Summit 2007 in the United Kingdom. Her research interests lie in the intersection of three fields of higher education: leadership, governance, and learning.

PRACTICAL LEADERSHIP IN COMMUNITY COLLEGES

Navigating Today's Challenges

I

LEADERSHIP ISSUES MANAGEMENT

Thinking About Leadership

Students of leadership theory have been able to follow the evolution of thinking about leaders, starting with the early belief that they are born with unique, undefined abilities that others simply do not have. After several years of studying leadership, scholars began to postulate that leaders possessed certain specific traits—such as high intelligence, creativity, and responsibility—at levels not found in other people. Then researchers developed the hypothesis that leadership traits were behavioral and could be developed. Contingency theory (also called *situational leadership*) advanced the notion that effective leadership behaviors were dependent upon what the situation called for (Hersey, 1984). Transactional and transformational theories of leadership examined the relationship between leaders and followers and the ability of leaders to motivate followers to make transformational changes (Bass, 1990). Bolman and Deal (1991) developed a framework for classifying leaders, arguing that leaders had strengths in one or more of four frames: structural, human resource, political, and symbolic. Leaders can use the frames as a way of assessing their strengths and the strengths and weaknesses of their leadership team. Several other assessments have been used to identify preferred individual and group leadership styles.

Kent Farnsworth (2007) applied the Greenleaf concept of servant leadership to higher education, arguing that leadership is essentially an act of service. Haden and Jenkins (2015) describe nine virtues of exceptional leaders. They make a case that the most effective leaders have in common the virtues of humility, honesty, courage, perseverance, hope, charity, balance, wisdom, and justice. Pairing practitioners and researchers, Campbell (1985) addressed community college leadership

[handwritten margin note:] Good leader: works ind from other problems/ solutions

in the areas of strategic planning, governance, finance, curriculum, human resources, technology, resource development, and public relations. Myron and colleagues (2003) examined the issues of transformational change, organizational design, policy development, student development, curriculum development and instructional delivery, workforce development, staff development, and resource development as they apply to leadership in community colleges. Also writing specifically for community colleges, Pamela Eddy (2010) made a case for viewing leadership from a multidimensional perspective: that a community college leader requires a variety of competencies—some skill based, some personality based, and others learned through experience. Eddy (2012) followed that publication with an issue of *New Directions in Community Colleges* that focused on the development, study, and implementation of the leadership competencies published by the American Association of Community Colleges in 2005 with support of the W. K. Kellogg Foundation. Roueche and Jones (2005) argued for the importance of entrepreneurial leadership and the willingness to take calculated risks to advance an institution, especially in an environment of declining public resources.

Scholars have studied leadership for a clear reason: it makes a difference. Byron McClenney, member of the Colorado Board for Community Colleges and Occupational Education and national director of leadership for Achieving the Dream (ATD), told George Boggs in a personal interview in 2011 that the ATD college coaches reached consensus on what matters the most in improving student success: leadership. The leadership that McClenney talked about was not only leadership on the part of the president, but also leadership at the board, faculty, and mid-level administrative levels.

The American Association of Community Colleges (AACC) published its list of competencies for community college leaders in 2005, with a second edition in 2013 (AACC, 2013). The AACC competencies have been studied extensively, and there have been no arguments about their appropriateness. The competencies listed in the revised version include organizational strategy; institutional finance, research, fundraising, and resource management; communication; collaboration; and advocacy. The curricula of leadership development programs and workshops should be reviewed to determine what skills and competencies they intend to develop. It is equally important for leaders to assess the competencies of their leadership teams and to provide development opportunities that build the skills needed to respond effectively to issues and to effect positive organizational change.

leaders: need to assess dev. opportunities to effect positive organizational change

In its most recent reports, *Reclaiming the American Dream: Community Colleges and the Nation's Future* (2012) and *Empowering Community Colleges to Build the Nation's Future: An Implementation Guide* (2014), AACC has laid out an ambitious agenda that requires strong college leadership and institutional transformation. The reports are a critical analysis of the colleges and call on college leaders to be more accountable for student success outcomes.

Although there has been a great deal of research about leadership in general, some publications dealing specifically with community college functions that require leadership, and competencies required for effective community college leadership, there has not been much focus on the practical issues that community college leaders face—often on a daily basis—and the impact that their responses can have. Leaders need to understand the different points of view that constituents bring to issues and how these issues can best be dealt with—or how an improper response can create significant problems for an institution and its leadership.

Thinking About Issues

The list of issues facing today's community college leaders is extensive: student unrest, racial and ethnic tensions, campus emergencies, guns on campus, safety and security, cybersecurity threats, increased calls for accountability, college completion rates, developmental education outcomes, athletic injuries, sexual assault, academic integrity, and many others. Leaders face a variety of circumstances that provide options to consciously or unconsciously respond. The situations in which leaders find themselves often lead to questions, challenges, or matters that can be contested. For the purposes of this book, leadership issues are matters that involve people—both internal and external to the campus—and their beliefs and values. Leaders need to understand that there can be legitimate differences of opinion about how the issues should be managed. Many of these issues can be dealt with by referring to existing policies, procedures, regulations, contracts, or laws. Others are more intricate and require careful thought and preparation. Community colleges are multifaceted, complex, and diverse organizations, and the issues faced by students, faculty, staff, administrators, and trustees are often both difficult and sensitive. There are many methods used to analyze leadership and styles of leadership, but the true test of a leader can best be measured by how the leader anticipates and manages the issues that emerge every day at every community college.

Origin of Issues

College issues frequently arise internally. They can be the result of an unexpected crisis, an accident, or interactions between and among students, faculty, and staff—or perhaps a difference of opinion in how a policy should be interpreted or how resources should be allocated. Divisions within the college, because of departmental structure or the separation of academic programs, technical programs, student services, and administrative services, are often sources of disagreement caused by differing perspectives. Personality, behavioral, and style differences can cause employment issues. Even such issues as assignment of offices or classroom space can cause dissention. Decisions by an administrator in one area of a college might create issues for administrators in another area. Perceptions of fairness—or lack of it—can affect campus climate. Administrators who want to respond quickly to a community or business need for a program might clash with faculty who want to move more slowly to ensure quality. Cultural or racial differences or insensitivities can lead to difficult and persistent issues. The negotiating strategies of employee unions and advocacy groups often create issues for college leadership.

College employees can best contribute to the success of the college when they receive proper orientation and are provided professional development opportunities that are aligned with the college's mission and vision. In too many instances, inadequate or misdirected orientation and development programs leave employees with an insufficient understanding of how their roles and the roles of other employees contribute to the overall college mission. This lack of understanding is often the source of internal issues that confront college leaders.

Sometimes issues emerge externally from the community, from local businesses, from city or county officials, or at the state or national levels. Community members might complain about noise coming from college facilities, traffic caused by the college, or students parking in residential areas. Business owners might ask the college to find better ways to meet their need for skilled workers, or they might complain about unfair competition from college food services, child care programs, or the college bookstore. State policy makers might make decisions that affect college funding or operations—or they may establish scorecards to publically highlight specific measures of college effectiveness. Accreditors might recommend changes in practices and policies or require the college to develop improved measures of student learning. National policy makers might challenge colleges to improve graduation rates or to lower loan default rates, or they make decisions to change regulations that affect colleges and their students. Foundations and the organizations they fund can challenge colleges to improve rates of student success in developmental and college programs. Relationships with the school districts that host concurrent enrollment programs or send graduates to the college can sometimes create issues for leaders. Challenges often originate from relationships with other higher education institutions that accept community college transfers or with the institutions that compete with community colleges for students.

Issues in the larger society often spill over to college campuses. Protests of the continued police shootings of African American males and the "Black Lives Matter" movement have led to racial demonstrations on campuses that are reminiscent of the student activism of the 1960s. In fact, the Higher Education Research Institute at the University of California at Los Angeles reported that the fall 2016 entering freshman class is the most likely to protest in half a century (Kueppers, 2016). Students are demanding more racial diversity in the faculty and leadership of colleges and the removal of symbols and names and images of college founders or former presidents whom they brand as racist. At the University of Missouri, the November 2015 student protests led to the resignation of the university president and chancellor. Shootings at campuses, such as the October 2015 attack at Umpqua Community College in Oregon, have raised renewed concerns about campus safety and security. Several states have passed legislation allowing guns on campuses, requiring leaders to address new concerns from faculty, staff, students, and parents. Terrorism and political posturing have led to concerns about tolerance and respect for people who have different religious beliefs.

Importance of Managing Issues

The health of any organization depends upon how effectively, efficiently, and consistently issues are managed. Issues that are allowed to linger often have a detrimental effect on the organization and its ability to function. Issues that are dealt with inconsistently or without explanation can adversely affect the morale of the organization's people. Clear institutional policies and procedures (and clear employee contract language in collective bargaining environments) are important tools to ensure that issues are handled fairly and consistently. However, there are times when issues are not covered by a policy or procedure or when they can be interpreted in more than one way. How leaders manage issues determines both their own effectiveness as leaders and the effectiveness of the organizations they lead.

Readers of this book will examine issues and how leaders manage them within the organizations they lead as well as those external issues that affect colleges, their students, and their employees. Effective issue anticipation, management, and response are critical skills for successful leaders in any organization. Although several typical and emerging issues are examined in this book, the exact nature of the issue is not as important as the specific skills that allow leaders and policy makers to manage effectively the diverse issues that are critical to fulfilling the institution's mission successfully.

For leaders, issues that require response and management are continually emerging and evolving. In this book, we encourage leaders to move beyond simply being responders to issues and instead study how to anticipate and manage issues effectively. Leaders need to think about how they might respond to an issue before they are faced with a potential crisis. Issues have interesting qualities and cycles, and their relative importance is open to individual interpretation. People who are affected by a challenge or problem that threatens an institution's ability to function effectively have many different perceptions and points of view. Differing opinions about issues may cause dissention within an organization and may even divert the focus away from the organization's primary mission. Each individual has a personal "construct" of an issue. How issues are viewed depends upon position, education, experience, beliefs, values, and myriad other factors. These different constructs present a significant challenge for leaders to take actions that will successfully move an issue to satisfactory resolution. Most often, for any issue, there are both pro and con sides. Sometimes, issues are multifaceted. It is critical to understand these varying viewpoints in formulating actions that will successfully move the issue forward.

Not only are issues continually changing, but also effective issue management challenges leaders to do things differently. Doing things differently within an organization challenges the status quo and is often met with resistance. The effective leader is able to navigate the issue to a resolution that is aligned with the overall mission of the organization.

A Model for Issue Management

Although leaders sometimes have to respond quickly to an issue, usually there is time to obtain valuable advice before deciding on a course of action. College administrators often seek the advice of advisory committees, cabinets, colleagues, personal coaches, or mentors. Leaders and students of leadership should review research reports, opinion editorials, or news articles about difficult issues. Leaders are wise to think about emerging issues that are reported in higher education news publications and to discuss them with their colleagues or leadership teams. Mock exercises or simulations that focus on how leadership would handle a similar situation can be valuable preparation for dealing with future issues.

practice + research

Written policies and procedures are helpful in deciding many issues. In all cases, it is important for a leader to be open-minded and respectful of all points of view, to have thought seriously about the legalities and ethics involved in issue management, and to know what line not to cross when deciding on a course of action. When issues are particularly complex and sensitive, a more systematic way of studying them, such as the model adapted from Bill Piland's unpublished doctoral student guide at San Diego State University outlined here, can be valuable. Students of leadership can use these steps to analyze leadership issues and decide how effectively they were managed and whether the issues could have been better managed differently. Leaders and leadership teams can make use of the steps to think about how issues should be managed.

1. **Identify the Issue.** Develop a concise written statement that specifically defines the issue. How important is the issue? How urgent is it? It is often valuable to check with others to see whether your definition of the issue matches theirs. Are there secondary or unspoken issues that might be important? Is the issue that you have identified the real issue, or is it a symptom of an underlying issue?

2. **Clarify the Issue.** Briefly describe the context in which the issue is being presented. Why is the issue emerging now? Is it related to other issues? What are the viewpoints or positions that exist concerning the issue (e.g., the pro and con sides to the issue). Are there more than two sides to the issue? How does the issue relate to the core values of the college? Why is managing the issue important?

3. **Analyze the Issue.** What are the viewpoints on the issue? Do people have differing views as to how the issue should be addressed? For each of the viewpoints you have identified, use the following questions to guide your analysis:

   a. *Identification of Viewpoint:* Describe each viewpoint. What are the positive and negative implications of each viewpoint?

b. *Recognition of Assumptions and Context:* What assumptions are being made by those who advocate for each viewpoint? What is the context in which each position is being presented? Was the viewpoint presented as a recommendation or a challenge? What level of training, experience, and background do the advocates for each viewpoint have? Where do the advocates work or study and what positions do they have? How do their positions and responsibilities affect their viewpoints? Where are the viewpoints presented (e.g., letter, email message, journal, newspaper, book, speech, demand list)? How did the issue emerge? Who received the arguments for the viewpoints (e.g., college leadership, board of trustees, general public)? How were the viewpoints presented (e.g. fact, theory, conjecture)? How do the assumptions identified help support or hinder acceptance of each viewpoint? How might your own assumptions affect your understanding or acceptance of the positions being presented?

c. *Analysis of Supporting Argument:* Do the advocates for the viewpoints provide logical arguments for the positions taken? Are the points made based on facts or opinions? Are the arguments for the position presented in a clear manner without straying to unrelated issues? Do others support the positions?

d. *Evaluation of Conclusions:* Are the conclusions clearly stated in the viewpoints presented? Are the conclusions consistent with the logic of the arguments presented? Are the conclusions directly related to the viewpoints?

e. *Courses of Action:* Do the advocates for the viewpoints provide any suggestions for actions that need to be taken to support the positions? Are the proposed actions consistent with the supporting argument and conclusions of each of the viewpoints? Are the suggested actions reasonable given the context of the issue presented? How aligned are they with the mission of the college and with student access, learning, and success? By addressing the issue, who will be affected and in what ways?

f. *Impact of Actions:* How well are the possible courses of action aligned with the college mission? How will a decision affect the college's people—in particular, students and their learning? How will the course of action affect college resources? What effect will it have on college facilities and safety and security for students and employees?

4. **Review Legal Implications.** Are there laws that come into play as this issue is being addressed? Will a decision create potential legal problems for the college or its people? Are there college policies or procedures that must be followed in addressing the issue?

5. **Review Ethical Implications.** Are there any ethical or moral implications involved in the issue? Will a decision that is aligned with a viewpoint compromise ethics or values? Is it an issue that involves fairness?

6. **Ensure Appropriate Processes Are Followed.** Is there time to involve appropriate college governance or administrative committees? Who should be informed that the issue is being addressed? What is the timeline for resolving the issue? Who will decide on a course of action (e.g., college president, department chair, dean, provost, vice president, board of trustees, state legislature, federal government)? Do you have the authority and responsibility to make the decision?

7. **State Your Position.** After listening, reading, and analyzing the various viewpoints presented on the issue, decide on a course of action. Use the following steps to support your position:

   a. Specifically state your position on the issue.

   b. Support your position using your analysis.

   c. What actions will you take as a result of your position?

8. **Communicate Your Position.** Communicate the position you have taken and why. Indicate your respect for individuals who have a different point of view. Is your decision final, or will you need endorsement of a higher-level administrator or a board of trustees? Determine the best method of communication. Should it be face to face or in writing? Ensure that all appropriate and interested parties are notified.

9. **Identify Leadership Implications.** Given the context of your decision, what are the implications for the college or district? How will your decision support the institutional mission; affect employee morale; and support student access, learning, and success? If the ultimate decision is to be made by others, how can you best present your point of view to the decision makers? If the decision is not one that you agree with, can you support it and help to make it work?

Life Balance

One of the most challenging aspects of community college leadership is that the issues cannot always be "turned off" when it is time to go home. Leaders often struggle to maintain balance in their lives. Although leaders generally have a high capacity for work, they also need time to maintain their personal and spiritual lives. Family relationships are particularly important. It is important for leaders to block out some time on their calendars for personal time and reflection. Sometimes, however, leaders have to make difficult choices between a work-related issue and personal events.

Anticipating Issues and Potential Outcomes

With experience in leadership and an understanding of organizational dynamics, it is often possible to foresee emerging issues and to take early action to address them at a stage that is less critical or troubling for the organization. Leaders can pick up on trends and concerns in informal discussions by attending meetings, reading meeting minutes, and by talking with students and members of the community. Serving on boards of community organizations provides a way to pick up on community concerns and to identify potential opportunities for the college. Reading daily education publications and newspapers can alert leaders about potential new requirements or regulations that can create issues for the college or its students. Attending state and national meetings and legislative or congressional hearings not only can alert leaders to potential issues but also can provide an opportunity to shape decisions that have the potential to create difficult issues for college leadership. Economic cycles present a classic case for issue anticipation. College leaders who foresee an economic downturn can act to prepare the college by making some decisions that minimize the negative consequences or make the resulting issues less severe.

Sometimes issues emerge without warning and do not provide a leader with an opportunity to take early action—and sometimes they are urgent and do not give leaders the time to consult with committees or colleagues. In these cases, it is important for leaders to have spent some time studying issues and case studies such as those discussed in this book. Thinking in advance about crisis management or dealing with unexpected issues will pay off when faced with a very real situation. Leaders should review case studies and practice simulations with their leadership teams so everyone has a common vision and set of values to deal with issues as they emerge.

Managing issues poorly or allowing them to linger can have a detrimental effect on a college. Sometimes poor management of an issue can be costly to the career of a college leader. At the same time, leaders who learn how to manage issues fairly and effectively and to maintain the trust of those they lead can have a significant and positive impact on a college and on the lives of the people they touch.

The issues, scenarios, and cases addressed in this book are based upon real situations. Often, they are emerging issues and issues that policy makers are struggling with, including emergency preparedness, data security, sexual harassment, college completion, developmental education, community college baccalaureates, performance-based funding, transfer barriers, proposed federal and state regulations, accreditation, rating of colleges, declining public support, diversity, equity, inclusion, civility, civil disobedience, academic freedom, governance, unions, votes of no confidence, organizational change, online classes, flipped classrooms, and many others.

Issues to Consider

A. In the fall of 2000, a janitor witnessed former Pennsylvania State University assistant football coach, Jerry Sandusky, performing oral sex on a young boy in a locker room on campus. Later that day, another janitor saw Sandusky showering with a boy who appeared to be twelve years old. The two staff members conferred with each another but told nobody else. They believed that if they reported the incidents they would be fired (Grasgreen, 2012). What can leaders do to create an environment on campus in which people feel safe enough to report bad news or inappropriate behavior? Were there mistakes in how the leadership at Penn State dealt with the crisis? _treat everyone at the same level of importance_

B. Two of the University of Missouri's top leaders resigned in November 2015 after student activists railed against what they saw as a divisive racial climate on campus. They accused the president of the university of not addressing racist and bigoted incidents. What should a leader do in response to racial, ethnic, or religious slurs? _address, free campus BUT in a respectful/academic_

C. Because some subjects discussed in college classes are sensitive and may cause significant levels of stress to some students, some college leaders are advocating the use of "trigger warnings" to give students prior notice of sensitive subjects. However, the use of trigger warnings is not universally accepted. In fact, conservatives are saying college is about confronting students with uncomfortable ideas to assist in the learning process. Do you think the use of trigger warnings is a good practice? What issues might be caused if college leaders advocated that these warnings should be noted in course syllabi? *No, anything can trigger anyone Professor should include in all syllabi*

Case Scenario

The chair of your college's counseling department informs you that she has heard that high school counselors are telling juniors and seniors not to consider attending a community college. She tells you that high school students are being told that community colleges are low-class institutions for losers. If students cannot be accepted by a major private university, they are told to apply to the nearest state university and to stay away from the local community college. High school publications indicate that 25 percent of graduating seniors are accepted directly into universities. No mention is ever made of how many graduates attend the local community college. What issues does the scenario create? What leadership competencies are involved? Who should be involved in addressing the situation? What actions would you take? Are there lessons to be learned?

REFERENCES

American Association of Community Colleges. (2012). *Reclaiming the American Dream: Community Colleges and the Nation's Future. A Report of the 21st-Century Commission on the Future of Community Colleges.* Washington, DC: Author. Retrieved from: http://aacc.wpengine.com/wp-content/uploads/2014/03/21stCenturyReport.pdf.

American Association of Community Colleges. (2013). *AACC Competencies for Community College Leaders* (2nd ed.). Washington, DC: Author. Retrieved from: http://www.aacc.nche.edu/newsevents/Events/leadershipsuite/Documents/AACC_Core_Competencies_web.pdf.

American Association of Community Colleges. (2014). *Empowering Community Colleges to Build the Nation's Future: An Implementation Guide.* Washington, DC: Author. Retrieved from: http://www.aacc21stcentury

center.org/wp-content/uploads/2014/04/EmpoweringCommunityColleges_
final.pdf.

Bass, B. M. (1990). *Bass & Stogdill's Handbook of Leadership Theory,
Research, and Management Applications* (3rd ed.). New York, NY:
Free Press.

Bolman, L., & Deal, T. (1991). *Reframing Organizations: Artistry, Choice, and
Leadership*. San Francisco, CA: Jossey-Bass.

Campbell, D. (1985). *Leadership Strategies for Community College Effectiveness*.
Washington, DC: American Association of Community Colleges.

Eddy, P. (2010). *Community College Leadership: A Multidimensional Model
for Leading Change*. Sterling, VA: Stylus.

Eddy, P. (2012). Leading for the Future: Alignment of AACC Competencies
with Practice. *New Directions for Community College* (No. 159).
San Francisco, CA: Jossey-Bass.

Farnsworth, K. (2007). *Leadership as Service*. Westport, CT: Praeger.

Grasgreen, A. (2012, July 13). Culture of Complacency. *Inside Higher Ed*.
Retrieved from: https://www.insidehighered.com/news/2012/07/13/
freeh-report-faults-penn-state-athletics-culture.

Haden, N., & Jenkins, R. (2015). *The Nine Virtues of Exceptional Leaders*.
Atlanta, GA: Deeds Publishing.

Hersey, P. (1984). *The Situational Leader*. New York, NY: Warner Books.

Kueppers, C. (2016, February 11). Today's Freshmen Class is the Most Likely to
Protest in Half a Century. *Chronicle of Higher Education*. Retrieved from:
http://chronicle.com/article/Today-s-Freshman-Class-Is/235273.

Myron, G., Baker, G., Simone, B., & Zeiss, T. (2003). *Leadership Strategies
for Community College Executives*. Washington, DC: Community
College Press.

Roueche, J., & Jones, B. (2005). *The Entrepreneurial Community College*.
Washington, DC: Community College Press.

How has the mission of community colleges changed over time?

2

MISSION

Questioning the Mission

The community college is an American innovation in higher education with origins dating to the late nineteenth century. Most historians point to the founding of Joliet Junior College in 1901 as the prototype of what would become the most democratic institution of higher education and postsecondary training in the world. Like Joliet, the early community colleges were extensions of high schools and were focused on preparing students to transfer to four-year universities. However, the mission of the community college has evolved over the years, shaped by societal and political pressures, and it continues to change. Today's community colleges are complex institutions with a broad range of educational, social, and economic functions. They have been frequently defined by their commitment to open access, convenience, and affordability. But in today's environment of declining resources and concern about student success, leaders are being forced to prioritize college offerings and functions.

Cohen and Brawer (2008) described community college missions by their functions of student services, career education, developmental education, community education, and the collegiate curricula in transfer and liberal arts. The development and history of community colleges include a remarkable growth in enrollment and an equally remarkable expansion of mission from a transition to upper-division college work that defined the earliest junior colleges to a comprehensive curriculum and the services required to meet the needs of diverse student populations and the local communities they serve. The 1947 landmark Truman Commission Report led to a dramatic expansion of community colleges and the democratization of higher education in the United States.

Some of the most debated and far-reaching issues in community colleges continue to be the compatibility and relative importance of their multiple missions (Ayers, 2005). Practitioners, researchers, and critics often have conflicting perspectives about the purpose and role of community colleges (Brint & Karabel, 1991; Dougherty, 1994; Jenkins & Cho, 2014; Pincus, 1980). Community college researchers categorize the colleges as nontraditional, nonspecialized by design, and mandated to provide a comprehensive curriculum to their communities (Ayers, 2005; Bailey & Morest, 2006; Beach, 2011; Vaughn, 2006). In contrast, practitioners are likely to focus on the ideals of the "open door," in particular, access to education and training programs, and responsiveness to community needs (Boggs, 1996, 2011, 2006; Shannon & Smith, 2006). Some researchers argue that the comprehensive mission of community colleges lacks sufficient focus, causing them to compete with numerous other organizations on multiple fronts (Alfred, 1998; Bailey, 2002; Quigley & Bailey, 2003). McPhail and McPhail (2006) argued that community college leaders must develop methods to prioritize their multiple missions in order to appropriately allocate fiscal resources and manage personnel. In fact, one outcome of the severe economic recession of 2008 in California was to give a higher priority to transfer, workforce, and basic skills education—and to direct funding away from avocational community service courses. Students were restricted in the number of times they could repeat courses, particularly in performing and visual arts and in physical education.

Aspects of the comprehensive mission have periodically come under criticism. In 1980, Fred L. Pincus wrote "The False Promise of Community Colleges: Class Conflict and Vocational Education," in which he criticized the increase in vocational offerings in community colleges. Pincus argued that the vocational programs were merely an educational tracking mechanism intended to maintain the economic class of their students. Similarly, Brint and Karabel (1991) claimed that the colleges were no longer primarily stepping stones to four-year colleges and universities. Instead, the authors suggested that community colleges were "vocationalizing" curricula and focusing on preparing students for work, thus limiting their opportunities for advancement in American society. Rhoades and Valdez (1996) contended that community colleges had too many missions and that maintaining all of them made it difficult to focus on emerging multicultural issues on campuses. They argued that community colleges had to find ways to integrate multicultural issues into their missions and in the way colleges conduct business.

John Levine (2000) conducted a qualitative, multiple-case study to define changes in the colleges' institutional missions during the 1990s. Though Levine's research results reported little change in institutions' missions during the 1990s, the data collected indicated alterations to missions to account for global economic concerns. Levine suggested that a new globally oriented vocationalism dominated the community college mission at the end of the twentieth century.

The expansion of the community college mission has not been without controversy, and the debates continue even today. In order to provide a basis for understanding mission issues, we provide a model for viewing the development of the community college mission in terms of generations, in which each generation builds upon the past and yet provides a new way of thinking about community colleges and what they do. Knowledge of these generations of the changing mission can be a valuable resource for the contemporary community college leader to guide discussions focused on setting priorities for college offerings and services.

Mission Generations

As the American community college sector evolved, the colleges modified or expanded their mission to meet the needs of a growing diverse student population and an increasingly complex society. This evolution, according to a study by Tillery and Deegan (1985), can be viewed in terms of the five generations of the American community college. The first generation, from 1900 to 1930, characterized community colleges as an "extension of secondary school." The focus during this generation was on helping high school graduates transition to higher education at a four-year college or university.

The second generation, from 1930 to 1950, is characterized as the "junior college generation." The mission focus in this generation is characterized by framing the identity of the community college as a higher education institution on its own by breaking away from the high school. There was also considerable attention paid to the development and role of local boards of trustees to define the community college's teaching and administration functions and to oversee the institutions.

Tillery and Deegan placed the third generation of community colleges in the time period from 1950 to 1970 and referred to this generation as the "community college generation." With impetus from the Truman Commission Report (1947), the term "community college" became popularized, and the growth of community colleges during this generation was dramatic. The mission of this generation of community colleges focused on expanding opportunity to higher education to people who would not have had a chance previously, including the large number of World War II veterans. Students were admitted to the community college with little or no attention to their level of academic preparation.

The fourth generation was referred to as the "comprehensive community college" and covered the period from 1970 to 1985. The major theme of the mission of the comprehensive community college was based on the needs of the community. In other words, the open-door mission opened access to the community college to a wide variety of learners, and leaders of the comprehensive community colleges reached out to the community to welcome everybody. While striving to be "everything to everybody," community colleges augmented their programs and services to create noncredit and community services classes. The comprehensive community college also began to experiment with nontraditional teaching practices and expanded occupational and technical programs to meet the needs of local employers. The taxpayer revolt that started in California with the passage of Proposition 13 in 1978 restricted public funding, shifted authority from local communities to the state level, and spread to other states. Limitations in funding support began to limit how comprehensive the community colleges could be.

Although Tillery and Deegan did not name the fifth generation, it is generally referred to as the "Contemporary Community College (mid-1980s to 1990). During this period, the mission focus was on using resources to respond to the needs of an ever-changing student population (Cohen & Brawer, 2008; Dougherty & Townsend, 2006; Levinson, 2005). Community colleges faced several key challenges: maintaining commitment to open-door practices, responding to diverse populations, and changing to respond to community needs and legislative mandates. In 1988, the American Association of Community Colleges' (AACC) Commission on the Future of Community Colleges had issued its report, *Building Communities: A Vision for A New Century*. Perhaps its most notable quote is, "We propose, therefore, that the theme 'Building Communities' become the new rallying point for the community college in America. We define the word 'community' not only as a region to be served, but also as a climate to be created."

What then is the sixth generation of community colleges? It may best be defined by what started as an effort by a single community college to define its vision for the future, an effort that grew into a movement that would reshape all of American higher education and bring national attention to student learning outcomes. After eighteen months of study and debate, Palomar College in Southern California released the report of its Vision Task Force. In the introductory letter in the spring of 1991, President George Boggs wrote:

Readers of these statements will note that they reflect a subtle but nonetheless profound shift in how we think of the college and what we do. We have shifted from an identification with process to an identification with results. We are no longer content with merely providing quality instruction. We will judge ourselves henceforth on the quality of student learning we produce. And further, we will judge ourselves by our ability to produce even greater and more sophisticated student learning and meaningful educational success with each passing year, each exiting student, and each graduating class. To do this, we must ourselves continually experiment, discover, grow, and learn. Consequently, we see ourselves as a learning institution in both our object and method. (Boggs, 1991)

Boggs wrote about the work of the Task Force in the AACC Chair's column in the *Community College Journal* in 1993 and called for a reinvention of community colleges and a change in the paradigm of how we think of community colleges (Boggs, 1993). In 1995, two members of the Palomar Vision Task Force wrote an article that served as a catalyst for higher education leaders to rethink teaching and learning. Barr and Tagg (1995), in a seminal article in *Change* magazine entitled, "From Teaching to Learning: A New Paradigm for Undergraduate Education," noted that colleges must take responsibility for learning at two distinct levels: institutional outcomes and individual learner outcomes. Barr and Tagg argued that the college's purpose is not to transfer knowledge but to create environments that bring students to discover and construct knowledge. A short time later, Boggs (1996) described the need to change the mission of community colleges in a mission-defining article entitled, "The Learning Paradigm" in the *Community College Journal,* where he examined the educational needs of contemporary society, suggesting that existing institutions have failed to adapt to the changing landscape. Boggs argued that educators must shift to a "learning paradigm" that centers all services on the learning needs of students and evaluates programs and personnel based on their contributions to student learning. In 1997, Terry O'Banion continued the learning paradigm conversation in his award-winning publication, *A Learning College for the 21st Century*, which defined a learning college as one that "places learning first and provides educational experiences for learners anyway, anyplace, anytime." Given the impact of the focus on learning outcomes instead of college processes, the sixth era of community colleges (1990–2000) can appropriately be called the "Learning College" generation. During this generation, the mission clearly emerged to focus on student learning and institutional outcomes.

In 2000, the American Association of Community Colleges, in partnership with Association of Community College Trustees, issued the report of its New Expeditions Initiative, *The Knowledge Net* (AACC, 2000). The report differed from the 1998 *Building Communities* report in several significant ways. In particular, community colleges were beginning to respond to the impact of three important societal forces: (1) the learning college movement, (2) the impact of globalization, and (3) the impact of the Internet.

Although attention to student learning outcomes continues through accreditation standards and association and college initiatives, the generation of community colleges that followed the learning college generation can perhaps best be called the "Entrepreneurial Community College." As economic support to community colleges was restricted, college leaders began to embrace entrepreneurial thinking even in the educational programs that the colleges provided. Evidence of emergence of the entrepreneurial type mission is noted in the founding of the National Association for Community College Entrepreneurship (NACCE) in 2002. It was founded as a nonprofit organization to serve the mission of accelerating entrepreneurship at community and technical colleges in the United States. The organization was established to serve two basic audiences: (1) community college administrators who manage entrepreneurship education programs and entrepreneurship centers, and (2) faculty members who teach entrepreneurship.

However, the college leaders were also encouraged to become more entrepreneurial themselves. Roueche and Jones (2006) showcased entrepreneurial leadership in their book, *The Entrepreneurial Community College*, which highlighted best entrepreneurial practices and introduced effective strategies for increasing revenue and reducing costs. Roueche and Jones identified trends that suggested that community colleges had developed entrepreneurial cultures. They observed that declining public resources, coupled with the demand that colleges do more with less, made it more of an imperative that entrepreneurism, flexibility, and adaptability thrive in the community college environment.

How has the community college mission changed since 2010? Although there have been changes, the shifts may not be as dramatic as one might think. The most apparent shift is the call for colleges to move beyond just providing access to accepting responsibility for the success of their students (Phillippe & Sullivan, 2005; Watson, Williams, & Derby, 2005). Community college educators are now encouraged to pay more attention to programs and services that focus on student success outcomes. Data on achievement gaps have focused attention on equity and diversity in college policies and practices (AACC, 2012; Center for Community

College Student Engagement [CCSSE], 2012; Complete College America, 2012; College Rewired, 2012). Demands from legislators for colleges to be more accountable have become ever more common. This shift to a focus on student completion is well documented and is the focus of the major reform initiatives and debates about who should attend community colleges, the curriculum, policies, and practices, even the degrees awarded by the community college (AACC, 2014; Erpenbach & Forte, 2007; Floyd et al., 2009; National Center for Education Statistics [NCES], 2004). All of these factors have created a complicated set of conditions that have coalesced around a single agenda: student completion of educational goals. The "Completion Agenda" refers to course, program, and degree completion and is driven by national, state, and local initiatives that are beginning to focus more on success of students than on access to education and training. It is the defining mission of the generation of community colleges since 2010. Community college leaders in the eighth generation of community colleges have had to react to the challenges inherent in the Completion Agenda while also dealing with many other issues.

Although some aspects of previous mission generations continue and blend into the next generation, the mission of community colleges has changed over time due to a variety of internal and external pressures and innovations in thinking. The mission continues to evolve. The following section of this chapter highlights some of the key mission-based pressures and challenges facing community colleges.

Given the economic and educational issues facing the United States, community colleges have never been more important (AACC, 2014; Floyd et al., 2009; Green, 2006). Community colleges face myriad economic, social, and political challenges, including declining state budgets, a greater emphasis on outcome-based accountability, competition from for-profit institutions, underprepared students, and a growing immigrant student population (AACC, 2012; Amey, Eddy, & Ozaki, 2007; Bailey, Badway, & Gumport, 2001; Jacobs & Dougherty, 2006; Levinson, 2005; Watson et al., 2005). Community college leaders must confront and overcome a host of challenges in the months and years ahead.

Completion Challenge

Not since the administration of President Harry S. Truman has the community college been the focus of such consistent attention from the president of the United States. On February 24, 2009, President Barack Obama challenged educators by declaring that "by 2020, America will once again have the highest proportion of college graduates in the world"

(The White House, 2009). This announcement, which fueled the Completion Agenda, was received with mixed emotions by various constituencies in the community colleges. The Obama administration, recognizing the economic imperative to educate and train our people, set aggressive goals for postsecondary attainment in the United States and emphasized the unique role that community colleges can play in achieving them (AACC, 2012; Gonzalez, 2010). Although some community college educators viewed a single-minded focus on completion as a threat to the open door, national associations, led by the American Association of Community Colleges, seized the opportunity to launch a united national Completion Agenda for community colleges.

In April 2010, the American Association of Community Colleges and five other community college organizations responded to President Obama's challenge, reaffirming their commitment to completion by issuing a joint statement, *Democracy's Colleges: Call to Action*. The other associations participating in the partnership were the Association of Community College Trustees, the Center for Community College Student Engagement, the League for Innovation in the Community College, the National Institute for Staff and Organizational Development, and Phi Theta Kappa. The associations also reaffirmed their commitment to increasing access and quality.

In the summer of 2011, AACC launched a new 21st-Century Initiative that began with a nationwide listening tour with stops at selected community colleges. A report, *Reclaiming the American Dream*, based on broad consensus findings from the listening tour, was completed in early 2012. The report emphasized several issues facing community colleges, including the need to reexamine the role, scope, and mission of the community college; and the existence of an "achievement gap" and need for "scalable proven practices" to respond to the needs of students. The report also suggested that community college educators must "redesign their institutions, their mission, and their students' educational experiences" to ensure that they meet the needs of a changing society.

Balancing Access and Success

Community colleges have successfully provided opportunity and access to higher education and training for millions of American citizens (Cohen & Brawer, 2008; Dougherty & Townsend, 2006; Horn, Nevill, & Griffin, 2006). Support of the open-access philosophy by policy makers has generally resulted in strong student demand at community colleges.

Community colleges must be committed to improving completion rates while maintaining or even increasing their commitment to access and quality. Recent reform initiatives have placed considerable pressure on community colleges to maintain the open door while focusing more deliberately on improving completion rates and overall institutional effectiveness (Boylan, 1999; Completion by Design, 2014; CCSSE, 2012; Jenkins & Cho, 2014; Lanty et al., 2009; Linn, 2004). Although there is no one-size-fits-all formula for balancing access and success, the current emphasis on completion will undoubtedly continue to influence programs, services, and administrative decisions by community colleges leaders.

Transition, Progression, and Transfer

The pathway to the community college from local high schools must be strengthened (Complete College America, 2012; Completion by Design, 2014; Davies, 1999; Handel, 2009; Horn et al., 2006). Many states and local school districts are increasingly more proactive in raising K–12 standards and boosting high school rigor. Although much attention has been placed on college-ready students, community colleges are now being challenged to examine their admissions and student support practices to be better prepared to support students transitioning from high school and those preparing to transition from community colleges to four-year colleges and universities (Davies, 1999; Completion by Design, MDRC, 2013). But how can transitions from high school to community college be improved? State policy makers have sought to better integrate the community college with K–12 school systems and state four-year colleges and universities.

Jenkins (2014) observed that deliberate pre-collegiate programs and strong student engagement efforts positively affect graduation and transfer rates at the community colleges. For example, in 2010, Harper College in Illinois and its local high school districts partnered to launch the Northwest Educational Council for Student Success to align curriculum and testing, expand dual-credit opportunities, and create career and academic pathways. As a result, high school students have earned hundreds of career certifications and completed several thousand dual-credit courses. Other notable efforts of effective community college and K–12 collaboration to improve college success and completion rates include the partnership between the Montgomery campus of the Lone Star College System with three local school districts that allows high schools to bus seniors to Lone Star's satellite center for training, leading to certificates in phlebotomy, advanced manufacturing, welding, and other areas while also earning high school credits. Folsom Lake College in California has a yearlong readiness program called College Connections that includes college preparation workshops for students on such topics as time management and career exploration, seminars for students and parents on financial aid, and a matriculation workshop to help students register for college.

Accreditation and Mission

The unique American system of institutional quality assurance is described in chapter 3. However, it is important to note here that all regional accreditation agencies require colleges to publish mission statements. The mission provides a framework for all institutional goals and activities. A college's mission statement is critical to any discussion of the college's regional accreditation reviews. Most important, the stated mission of the institution is the very first criterion or standard in each of the regional accrediting agencies. In some regions, accrediting commissions ask colleges to explain how the mission is used to guide the college's programs and practices.

Push from the For-Profit Sector

For-profit postsecondary education providers encompass a wide range of institutions. They offer associate, baccalaureate, master's, and sometimes doctoral education and training, in addition to certificates and diplomas. They are accredited by either national or regional accrediting agencies. The majority of them offer courses online as well as in person. Zinshteyn (2014), program manager for the Education Writers Association, reported that for-profit colleges and universities have grown in presence in American higher education. According to Zinshteyn, the sector accounted for an estimated 13 percent of all US college students in 2009—up from 5 percent in 2001. The students who are attracted to the for-profit sector are the same types of students who traditionally attend the community college. According to Bailey and colleagues (2010), African Americans accounted for 22 percent of the enrollment of for-profit institutions, compared with 14 percent at two-year public colleges and 11 percent at four-year public colleges. Fifteen percent of students in for-profits were Hispanic, compared with nearly 16 percent at two-year and 10 percent at four-year public colleges. About 65 percent of students in for-profit institutions were twenty-five years and older, compared with 31 percent at four-year public and 40 percent at two-year public colleges. And about two-thirds of students at for-profits were female compared to 57 percent at public community colleges. Bailey and colleagues (2010) observed that community college leaders and staff do not perceive for-profits as a competitive threat. The researchers also noted that community college leaders might learn from the for-profits' emphasis on customer service, employment placement support, and degree completion rates.

Technological Development

There is an increase in demand for higher education, and community colleges that are flexible enough to incorporate the latest hardware and software will be better equipped to increase educational access because technological developments are stimulating new ways of thinking about educational service delivery (Mars & Ginter, 2007). Although institutions of all types and sizes can expect to experience change as environmental factors intensify and technology advances accelerate, community colleges, perhaps more than any other sector of higher education, may be uniquely positioned to use technology as a management tool for the future (Stewart, 2008). Community colleges led the rest of higher education in finding ways to serve nontraditional students with individual needs and in considering technological solutions for enhancing quality, expanding access, improving success rates, and containing cost through improved productivity. Community colleges must have a strong technology planning process that routinely and consistently engages all stakeholders (EDUCAUSE, 2015; Stewart, 2008). The president of the college and the entire leadership team must strive to keep the technology infrastructure aligned with the mission, vision, and goals of the college.

Legislative Mandates

Recently the nation's community colleges have been bombarded with reform initiatives. Most of the legislated or regulatory reform is not voluntary but mandated at the state level. For example, several state governments have legislated the use of standardized tests to measure community college performance and to provide data for accountability (Bailey, 2009). Such legislation has enormous ramifications for institutional planning and resource allocation. States are debating additional educational reforms. Some are calling on high schools to make changes in graduation requirements. Recently, Indiana lawmakers approved a bill directing the K–12 sector to identify students who may need remedial classes in college and help them before they leave high school. Some states are requiring colleges to provide extra support to high school students who take college classes for credit. High school enrichment advocates claim that such an approach will help more students finish college by shortening the path to graduation. Florida lawmakers approved legislation that allowed many students at the state's public community colleges to skip developmental classes and immediately enroll in college-level courses even if they are not prepared for college-level work. The lawmakers in Colorado passed legislation to allow public four-year colleges to place borderline students into regular credit-bearing classes while providing them with additional support. Previously, the four-year colleges in Colorado were required to redirect underprepared students to community colleges for remedial classes.

In 2011, Texas lawmakers took bold steps to improve student success when they approved legislation that required colleges to base developmental coursework on research-based best practices. The law also allowed colleges to exempt students in developmental education courses from paying tuition and required them to develop a plan for developmental education. Connecticut's law challenged public colleges to integrate developmental education into regular credit-bearing courses. In addition, the Connecticut legislation placed limitations on how many remedial courses per semester a student can take and required the public colleges to use more than a single assessment measure, such as a placement test, to determine whether students needed extra support to be successful. Some community college educators and researchers question whether scaling back remedial education as is being done in Connecticut and Florida could leave some students unprepared and decrease their chances of success (Beach, 2011; Center for Research on Learning and Teaching, 2009; Linn, 2004; Szelenyi & Chang, 2002).

Funding the Mission

Issues of finance and the economy are covered in chapter 4. However, it would be a mistake to ignore the effect that funding issues have on the community college mission. State and federal legislation have a dramatic effect on mission. Examples include limitations on financial aid, elimination of funding for undocumented immigrant students and classes taught to the incarcerated, limitations on property taxes rates and tuition charges, and legislation on college enrollment priorities. During the economic downturn of the late 2000s, California directed community colleges to give priority to funding academic, workforce, and developmental education programs and to cut funding to community services courses.

Because of funding limitations, many community colleges struggle to maintain a balanced full-time to part-time faculty ratio. Declining public investment in community colleges at the state level stimulates college responses that may affect core programs and, therefore, the mission of community colleges. Further, especially since 2000, community college leaders have been encouraged to aggressively pursue external funding sources. Indeed, AACC (2014) has listed resource development as a key leadership competency for community college leaders. The present-day community college leader is expected to engage in private development efforts, innovative financial aid solutions, and new student tuition structures to ensure quality public higher education (Heaton, 2015). The mission of the community college is necessarily altered by unfunded program development and declining general fund budgets.

Workforce Preparation Issues

Despite the current attention being paid to the Completion Agenda, many community colleges have not clearly identified the role that workforce preparation plays in their completion efforts. Community college leaders face a dilemma when it comes to a choice of focusing either on (a) increasing completion rates using traditional measures (that is, attainment of associate's and bachelor's degrees) or (b) getting people back to work with certificates and industry credentials that are not counted by the government as success measures. However, in spite of earlier concerns about tracking students, there exists a clear sense of urgency for community colleges to focus on workforce preparation along with the traditional academic programs at the college. Does emphasis on workforce preparation threaten liberal arts? On the surface, it may appear to be the case because traditional community college instructional models and curricula are not designed to facilitate the integration of workforce preparation and academic programs. Jacobs (2000, 2006) suggested that it is time for community colleges to focus not only on traditional academic and workforce programs, but also on short-term, work-related certificates in specific programs. Focusing solely on the traditional programs narrowly defines student success while overlooking the needs and achievements of a significant number of people, disenfranchising large numbers of community college students.

Developing Partnerships

Partnerships with businesses have the potential to become an institution-transforming catalyst in community colleges. Business and postsecondary education have found common cause in recent decades in the preparation of a skilled workforce to preserve the nation's competitiveness in response to rapid technological changes and increasing global competition. Community college leaders need to systematically partner with the pre-K–16 systems so that federal, state, district, and postsecondary programs work together to support earning a degree or certificate. We need seamless articulation between high schools and community colleges—and between community colleges and universities. Further, community college–industry partnerships can provide impetus for transformation in higher education. Community colleges are well positioned to improve postsecondary attainment for many Americans. But they must find ways to integrate their three missions of academic transfer, occupational education, and developmental education in order to improve student success and accomplish that goal.

Curricular Reform

In order to be competitive, community colleges will need to improve educational services by revising curricula and adopting new technologies (AACC, 2014). The values underlying teaching and learning need to be critically examined. New pedagogy is needed for teaching students how to successfully manage changing environments (Barr & Tagg, 1995; Gross, 1999; Lorenzo & LeCroy, 1994). This emphasis on "outcomes-based learning" shifts the learning paradigm from being behaviorally oriented to being developmentally oriented (Shipley, 1995). The goal is to move students from just accomplishing discrete tasks to knowing how to accomplish those tasks.

Developmental education is increasingly the focus of reform efforts. Developmental education classes are those that are below college level. Students pay tuition and can use financial aid for remedial courses that prepare them for college-level work, but they do not receive college credit. Most remediation occurs in reading, writing, and math (Bailey, 2009; Boyland, 1999). Within and among community colleges, *remedial* often is used interchangeably with the terms *developmental* and *basic skills*. We use the term *developmental education* for all community college classes below college-level. Community colleges use a variety of methods to determine which students are placed in developmental education. Some use national college admissions exams, such as the ACT or SAT, to determine whether students are eligible to enroll in college-level courses. Other institutions require students to take a placement exam, such as Accuplacer or COMPASS, before they register for courses. Typically, students are given a list of the courses they should take based on their performance on the placement test. However, many students who are referred to developmental education never enroll in it. Many who complete one remedial course fail to show up for the next course in the sequence. Overall, fewer than one half of students who are referred to developmental education complete the recommended sequence (Complete College America, 2012; College Rewired, 2012; MDRC, 2013). The evaluation data concerning developmental education are equally discouraging. Much of the research on developmental education is suggestive of success but cannot reliably measure the effect of remediation or differentiate among different approaches (Boylan, 1999). The handful of more definitive studies shows mixed results at best (MDRC, 2013). Community colleges throughout the nation are aggressively searching for better ways to address the needs of the underprepared. Some of those efforts are based on curriculum reform and course redesign.

The Carnegie Foundation for the Advancement of Teaching is sponsoring one of the most promising reforms of developmental mathematics, devising two new pathways for developmental mathematics students: Statway and Quantway. Both pathways aim to accelerate students' progress through their developmental mathematics sequence and through a college-level course for credit. The two pathways also present engaging, relevant, and useful mathematics concepts that students can use in their daily lives. Statway and Quantway are taught using common curricula, assessments, online platform, and innovative instructional approaches.

A college's curriculum conveys implicit values and institutional priorities. Some community college practitioners have responded to changing student demographics by incorporating diverse values and literatures into their curricula and by acknowledging new research on students' learning styles and needs for support services (Gross 1999; Harris & Kayes, 1995; Terryll-Powell & Barnett, 2003). The community college curriculum may be permanently changed by today's economy and political climate. Limited funding, the pressure for accountability, changing student demographics, and the public's lack of trust in the higher education enterprise are affecting the operations, programs, and services of the contemporary community college (Levine, 2004; McPhail, 2004).

More and more community colleges are restructuring their curricula to more accurately meet the needs of the local economy. Community colleges are shifting their traditional curricula in order to address local job loss challenges. This shift is evident in community colleges such as Macomb Community College in Michigan, where former autoworkers seek programs to gain new job skills. In other locations, community colleges and state governments have collaborated to develop programs to retrain unemployed workers.

Metropolitan Community College (MCC), located in Omaha, Nebraska, established a new two-year program for data center management. With this new forum, MCC will have a program based on real-world working conditions in a modern data center that includes heterogeneous systems from numerous IT hardware and software vendors.

The shifts in curricula to meet workforce demands directly affect the mission of community colleges. Gone are the days when local community colleges could offer every possible program that faculty wanted to teach or students desired. Colleges are making choices and prioritizing the curriculum offerings.

The 2014 passage of Proposition 30 in California provided nearly $200 million more to the state's community colleges, according to a *Los Angeles Times* report. The additional money was much needed for a system that had been forced to cut class offerings significantly and even turn away students in an effort to balance dwindling budgets. The state's plan for college reform accompanied the additional funding. The reforms were designed to improve completion rates and accessibility throughout the system. McPhail and McPhail (2006) suggested that by prioritizing programs and services, college leaders are better positioned to more effectively serve their students and communities. Community colleges are transforming their curricula and services to meet today's economic and societal demands.

Community College Baccalaureates

As jobs evolve to require more technical training, new pressures emerge to meet the need to improve educational attainment, and the costs of higher education continue to escalate, more states are expanding the mission of community colleges. With all of the reform and accountability issues affecting them, is the community college baccalaureate a logical evolution of the mission or a threat to it? Over the past two decades, the number of community colleges authorized to offer bachelor's degree programs has steadily risen. Though still confined to a very small number of institutions and limited degree programs, this phenomenon continues to generate widespread attention and controversy (Floyd & Walker, 2008;

Levine, 2004). The trend toward the community college baccalaureate not only expands and potentially challenges the traditional mission of two-year colleges; it also has the potential to threaten the relationships between the two- and four-year sectors of higher education. Twenty-two states have now authorized community colleges to offer baccalaureates, usually in applied programs not offered by the public university systems. In most cases, the colleges have maintained a primary focus on a traditional community college mission, even though the colleges have often changed their names, dropping the word *community* and sometimes adding the word *state* in response to requirements from accreditors or incentives from state government. In a few cases, community colleges have been completely transformed into four-year institutions. Examples include the transformation of Westark Community College into the University of Arkansas at Fort Smith and Utah Valley Community College into Utah Valley University.

Organizations and Initiatives

Several organizations have developed initiatives, often with foundation funding, that are affecting practices that have the potential to affect mission. The most noteworthy are Complete College America, Achieving the Dream, Completion by Design, the Community College Survey of Student Engagement, and the Community College Completion Corps.

Complete College America was established in 2009. It is a national nonprofit with a single mission: to work with states to significantly increase the number of Americans with quality career certificates or college degrees and to close attainment gaps for traditionally underrepresented populations. Complete College America believes there is great reason for optimism and a clear path forward if significant changes are made to higher education practices. The organization espouses five student success drivers: strengthening developmental education, performance funding, co-requisites, full-time attendance, and structured scheduled guided pathways. Thirty-three states and the District of Columbia have pledged to work with Complete College America to improve college completion rates.

The Achieving the Dream National Reform Network (ATD) is intended to help more community college students succeed. The Lumina Foundation and seven founding partner organizations launched the network in 2004. Achieving the Dream now leads the most comprehensive nongovernmental reform movement for student success in higher education history. ATD is guided by five principles: committed leadership, use of evidence to improve programs and services, broad engagement, systemic institutional improvement, and accountability for equity. As of 2015, more than two hundred institutions of higher education, one hundred coaches and advisors, fifteen state policy teams, and numerous investors and partners working throughout thirty-four states and the District of Columbia make up the ATD network.

Completion by Design is a Gates Foundation–funded initiative that involves cadres of community colleges within the states of Florida, North Carolina, and Ohio that are working to assist large groups of students to succeed by developing coherent pathways of study while containing college costs, maintaining open access, and ensuring the quality of college programs and credentials. Completion by Design has identified three key completion goals on which to focus: earning certificates and degrees, transferring to four-year institutions, and raising the value of completers in the labor market.

The Community College Survey of Student Engagement, a product and service of the Center for Community College Student Engagement, is a well-established enterprise that helps institutions to focus on good educational practice and to identify areas in which they can improve their programs and services for students. Administered during the spring mostly to returning students, CCSSE asks about institutional practices and student behaviors that are highly correlated with student learning and retention. The Survey of Entering Student Engagement (SENSE) helps colleges focus on students' experiences in the critical first few weeks of college. Grounded in research about what works in retaining and supporting entering students, SENSE collects and analyzes data about institutional practices and student behaviors. College leaders can use data from the surveys to launch college improvement initiatives.

Phi Theta Kappa Honor Society recognizes community college students who have achieved academic excellence. Phi Theta Kappa was the only student organization invited to sign Democracy's Colleges: Call to Action with the major community college associations in 2010. Phi Theta Kappa sponsors the Community College Completion Corps and has developed a comprehensive toolkit for its chapters to use in planning a "Signing Day for the Call to Action in Support of Students." Through the Community College Completion Corps, students sign a commitment to complete their programs and to assist other students to complete. Further, Phi Theta Kappa has also developed a unique transfer tool, CollegeFish .org, available now to all members and in the early stage of being positioned as a resource for all community college students. CollegeFish.org matches students to the transfer institution that best meets their needs, keeps them informed about upcoming deadlines, monitors transfer credits, and provides information about financial aid and scholarships. Research has shown that Phi Theta Kappa members are significantly more likely to complete a degree than other students with similar grade point averages (Fain, 2016).

In response to President Obama's completion challenge for community colleges to educate an additional 5 million students to achieve degrees, certificates, or other credentials by 2020, the American Association of Community Colleges is leading the advancement of the next era of community college evolution through its three-phase 21st-Century Initiative. The 21st-Century Commission report, *Reclaiming the American Dream, Community Colleges and the Nation's Future: A Report from the 21st-Century Commission on the Future of Community Colleges*, and the 21st-Century implementation report, *Empowering Community Colleges to Build the Nation's Future: An Implementation Guide*, are available in the 21st Century Center (http://www.aacc.nche.edu).

AACC is also coordinating a national partnership to build capacity for community colleges to implement a pathways approach to student success and college completion. Partners include Achieving the Dream, the Aspen Institute, the Center for Community College Student Engagement, the Community College Research Center, Jobs for the Future, the National Center for Inquiry and Improvement, and Public Agenda. The partners selected thirty community colleges to participate and also are substantively involved in designing and delivering a model series of six two-day pathways institutes, each focusing on key elements of a fully scaled pathway model for community colleges. The project is funded through a $5.2 million grant from the Bill & Melinda Gates Foundation.

The attention to pathways for students was stimulated by the studies and publications done by the Community College Research Center at Teacher's College, Columbia University. In particular, the publication *Redesigning America's Community Colleges*, by Bailey, Jaggars, and Jenkins (2015), criticizes community colleges for insufficient student guidance through the maze of course offerings, referring to the colleges as "cafeteria colleges." The authors call for more structured pathways that help students to succeed.

Middle College High Schools (MCHSs)/Early College High Schools are located on college campuses and aim to help students complete high school and encourage them to attend college. Although Middle College High Schools, such as the one at LaGuardia Community College in New York, have been in existence since the 1970s, there has been a recent resurgence in the growth of the programs. The programs offer a project-centered, interdisciplinary curriculum with an emphasis on team teaching, individualized attention, and the development of critical thinking skills. Students are also offered support services, including specialized counseling, peer support, and career experience opportunities. The Middle College National Consortium is an organization representing more than fifty public schools on college campuses across the nation. It is composed of Middle and Early College high schools (which are high school–college partnerships) and school districts in sixteen states committed to preparing students from underserved communities for college by giving them rigorous coursework that will lead to college credits while these students are still enrolled in high school (Middle College National Consortium, n.d.).

In recent years, some Middle College High Schools have converted to the Early College High School model, which offers students a five-year accelerated course of study during which they can earn an associate degree or two years of college credits in addition to a high school diploma. Students identified as at-risk by their teachers and counselors attend MCHSs and are encouraged to succeed at high school and go on to higher education or advanced training through peer modeling (students enrolled at the college), small classes, and superior academic support services (Lieberman, 2004). The Bill & Melinda Gates Foundation, along with Carnegie Corporation of New York, the Ford Foundation, and the W. K. Kellogg Foundation, started the Early College High School Initiative in 2002. The initiative was established to redesign 150 early college high schools for underserved and low-income young people and neighborhoods over five years. Jobs for the Future (JFF) coordinates the initiative.

Given today's demands, the need for private support to augment the community colleges' operating budgets in order to implement reform initiatives has never been greater. For the first time in the history of community colleges, major foundations have paid attention to the increasing challenges facing the sector. The fact that community colleges educate half of the undergraduate students in the nation served as a catalyst for this newfound attention. Specifically, the Bill & Melinda Gates and the Lumina foundations have helped significantly to support community colleges in their efforts to respond to the Completion Agenda. The Bill & Melinda Gates Foundation has done much to orchestrate that new era of relationships between foundations and community colleges. The Gates Foundation has funded programs designed to reform higher education such as Completion by Design. According to the *Chronicle of Higher Education*, since 2006, Gates has spent $472 million to remake US higher education (Parry, Field, & Supiano (2014). The *Chronicle* reported that $343 million of the Gates funds were spent since January 2008. Lumina Foundation, the other significant funder of community college reform efforts, espouses the value that education provides the basis for individual opportunity, economic vitality, and social stability. Lumina's overarching goal is to increase the higher education attainment rate of the United States to 60 percent by 2025.

Reform Effectiveness

Evaluations of the effectiveness of developmental education reform efforts are not yet definitive enough to suggest that one intervention is more effective than another. However, research studies have identified some useful innovative methods that show promise of improving developmental education outcomes. These include accelerated courses, learning communities, enhanced student support, accelerated learning, and combined courses.

Students can complete their remedial courses at a faster pace by taking accelerated courses. At the Community College of Denver, for example, students in the FastStart program take two semesters of remediation in one semester. The program provides students with extra supports, such as a required weekly study group. Students in FastStart have greater academic success than remedial students who are not in the program.

Kingsborough Community College in New York has had success with a learning community program in which a group of freshmen take three classes together: remedial English, a college-level course, and a student success course (an orientation-type class that provides tips on time management, how to study, and how to use campus resources). By taking several classes with the same group, students have an opportunity to befriend and support one another. The extra academic and social supports that learning communities provide can have positive effects. Students who participated in the Kingsborough learning community were more likely than nonparticipants to take and pass the English skills assessment tests necessary to enroll in college-level English. Long-term studies at various community colleges, including Community College of Denver, North Seattle Community College, and the QUANTA program at Daytona Beach Community College in Florida, suggest that students in learning communities have significantly higher retention, persistence, and graduation rates than students in traditional courses.

Research (MDRC, 2013) suggests that students who test just below college-ready can be successful in college-level courses, especially if extra academic support—such as tutoring and group study time—is incorporated into the class. The Community College of Baltimore's Accelerated Learning Project places borderline remedial English students into college-level English. To provide extra support, the project requires students to take an additional course that serves as a study hour for the English class. The same professor teaches both courses. A study by the Community College Research Center found that students in the program were more likely to pass the first two college-level English courses (English 101 and 102) than students not in the program.

Washington's Integrated Basic Education and Skills Training (I-BEST) program has become a national model for helping students who test into the lowest levels of remediation earn a job-related credential. The program is particularly effective for adult basic education students and English language learners. I-BEST students' curriculum combines basic skills education with college credit, career-training courses. Early data show that I-BEST students are more likely to earn a job-related credential than similar students not enrolled in the program.

A Framework for Mission Management

Mission management is a process that has concrete steps and requires college team members to analyze the internal and external factors that affect the institution. The team defines the procedures and steps the college will take to achieve the defined goals and objectives. Figure 2.1 highlights the seven components of our conception of a mission management framework.

1. **Assess Community Needs.** Assessing societal needs and expectations is the first step in undertaking mission management. Community colleges face increasing pressure to respond to shifting societal trends. A community needs assessment identifies the strengths and resources available in the community to meet the needs of the college's constituencies (Coman & Ronen, 2009; University of Kansas Work Group for Community Health and Development, 2010). A community assessment may be limited to a compilation of demographic data from census records, results of surveys conducted by others, and informal feedback from community partners. Or assessments may be expanded to include focus group discussions, town meetings, interviews with stakeholders, and telephone or mailed surveys to partnership members and the community.

Figure 2.1   Mission Management Process

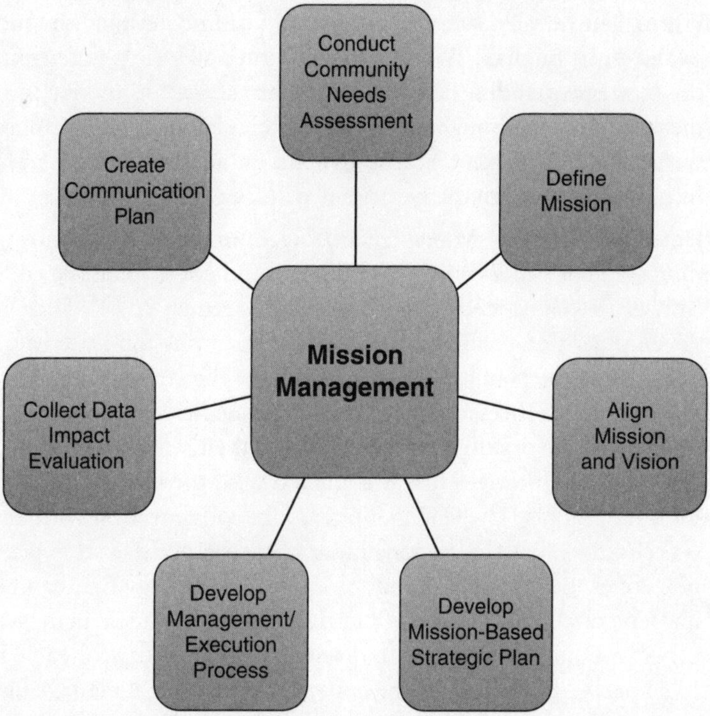

2. **Develop the Right Mission Statement.** Leaders should emphasize the current mission statement to employees, which clarifies the purpose and primary, measurable objectives of the organization (Bryson, 2004; Bryson & Alston, 2005). A mission statement is meant to be used by leaders to guide the current and future direction of the college.

3. **Align the Vision Statement with the Mission Statement.** Although mission statements define an institution's purpose, vision statements help to describe the organization's direction. Vision statements also include the college's values and goals. Vision statements give direction for employee behavior and help provide inspiration. The institution's vision statement should also help inspire the external community to work with the college.

4. **Develop a Mission-Based Strategic Plan.** Once the leader has collaborated with constituent groups to establish a clear mission and vision, a strategic plan can be developed. A good strategic plan

includes specific, short-term goals covering all the areas that need improving in order for the leader to provide oversight to attain the vision. The organization's mission and vision determine the success of the strategic plan. Without the mission and vision statements, the strategic plan has no ultimate goal to strive for and lacks measurability. Although an institution can have a strategic plan without a mission or vision statement, implementing such a plan is likely to be problematic because it will lack direction.

5. **Develop a Strategic Management/Execution Process.** The strategic management process involves defining and controlling the college's future, as well as its current status (Rothaermel, 2012). The development of a shared vision statement, a mission statement, and a strategic plan are the foundation of the strategic management process. Having clearly defined the vision and mission of the organization, leaders can then set strategic operational objectives that are aligned with the institution's long-term goals. The leadership team, in collaboration with key stakeholders, has the responsibility to translate these strategic objectives into an operational or execution strategy that can be implemented, monitored, and evaluated. The strategic management process requires the leader to delegate responsibility for each goal to a specific individual at the college. This strategic management process also defines the number of employees, the budget, and other resources that must be used to complete the task.

6. **Collect Data and Evaluate Impact.** Collecting and interpreting useful data is an essential step community college leaders can take to implement effective leadership practices. Community colleges usually collect vast amounts of valuable data that can be used to track the progress and performance of their students. However, because institutional research is frequently underfunded and relatively undeveloped at many community colleges, data remains underutilized to inform decision-making and practices (Calderon & Mathies, 2013). In today's data-informed environment, colleges need proof to show whether the institution and its practices are effective or not.

7. **Develop a Strategic Communication Process.** Strategic communication helps the leader share a clearly defined message with everyone involved with the institution—internally and externally (Keyton, 2011). The development of a strategic communication plan should be a top priority for the president and

the leadership team. The communication plan must outline an intentional process that defines what each constituent group within the institution needs to hear from the president and other leaders. A communication plan is a written document that describes the following: (1) what the leader wants to accomplish (objectives); (2) ways in which those objectives can be accomplished (goals or outcomes); (3) the audience that will address how objectives will be accomplished (the tools and timetable), and (4) how progress will be measured (evaluation). Although investing time and resources in strategic planning is critical to achieving the institution's vision, mission, and goals, a communication plan drives the execution. The best time for an administrator to develop a communication plan is now. The communication plan is informed by the mission and vision, an inventory of existing communications, constituent groups, and subordinates. It helps to keep the administrators focused on the goals and objectives throughout the year (Moorcroft, 2003). Communication is not a one-time event; it is ongoing all the time. It helps everyone at the institution remain aware of priorities and protects the administrators from last-minute demands for information, and it reduces confusion and guessing about what is taking place at the institution.

Leaders need to establish measurable milestones along the path to the institutional vision. The mission management process involves defining and controlling the college's future as well as its current status. Thus, community college leaders must constantly reinforce the mission and vision of the college instead of only once or twice a year when they are updating the strategic plan.

Issues to Consider

A. Was California correct in setting a higher priority on funding transfer education, vocational education, and developmental education while cutting support for community education? How does prioritization of functions affect the historical community college mission?

B. When funding is restored to a college after an economic recession, how should the college leadership decide where the restored funding should go? Should programs that were cut back or eliminated be restored, or should increased funding go to other programs or new initiatives?

C. The American Institutes for Research released a study of early college high schools in 2013 (DeSantis, 2013). The report demonstrated that students who attend early college high schools that are located on community college campuses and that offer students a chance to earn credit toward a college degree while they finish high school are more likely than are their peers to graduate, enroll in college, and earn an associate degree. However, Matt Reed issued a warning to his colleagues who might be considering the establishment of an early college high school (Reed, 2013), saying that some faculty will oppose it because they see it as a threat to the status of their professions, an encroachment by high schools onto college territory, and an implied insult. Do early college high schools belong on community college campuses? Should a leader get faculty buy-in before implementing an early college high school? How would you deal with this issue?

D. Should more community colleges be authorized to offer baccalaureates? What issues are created regarding faculty credentials, accreditation, and relationships with other educational institutions? How does the mission of the community college change when it offers a baccalaureate? Are there safeguards that can be put in place to retain important components of the community college mission when it begins to offer a more advanced degree?

E. Will policies that limit the amount of development education that community colleges offer (as has happened in Connecticut) or giving students the option not to enroll in developmental education (as has happened in Florida) effectively increase student completion rates? What are the advantages and disadvantages of these policies?

F. How are the current community college reforms at the state and national levels impacting the mission at the community college? Is it likely that efforts to increase completion rates will affect the historical open-access mission of the community college? What safeguards can community college leaders put in to place to ensure that community colleges remain accessible to all students in need of the opportunities available at public higher education institutions?

Case Scenario

You receive a letter from the president of the nearest state university, the major transfer institution for your students. The letter informs you that, because of state funding reductions, the university will be limiting the number of transfer students it admits so that it can preserve seats for deserving freshmen. In addition, the grade point average for students transferring from community colleges will be increased from 2.75 to 3.25 beginning next fall semester. What issues does the scenario create? What leadership competencies are involved? Who should be involved in addressing the situation? What actions would you take? Are there lessons to be learned?

REFERENCES

Alfred, R. (1998). From Closed Doors to Open Systems: New Designs for Effectiveness in Community Colleges. *Journal of Applied Research in the Community College, 5*(1), 9–19.

American Association of Community Colleges. (1988). *Building Communities: A Vision for a New Century: A Report of the Commission on the Future of Community Colleges.* Washington, DC: Author.

American Association of Community Colleges. (2000). *The Knowledge Net: A Report of the New Expeditions Initiative.* Washington, DC: Author.

American Association of Community Colleges. (2012, April). *Reclaiming the American Dream: A Report from the 21st Century Commission on the Future of Community Colleges.* Washington, DC: Author. Retrieved from: http://www.aacc.nche.edu/21stCenturyReport.

American Association of Community Colleges. (2014). *Empowering Community Colleges to Build the Nation's Future: An Implementation Guide.* Washington, DC: Author. Available at www.aacc21stcenturycenter. org.

Amey, M. J., Eddy, P. L., & Ozaki, C. C. (2007). Demands for Partnership and Collaboration in Higher Education: A Model. *New Directions for Community Colleges, 2007*(139), 5–14. doi: 10.1002/cc.288.

Ayers, D. F. (2005). Neoliberal Ideology in Community College Mission Statements: A Critical Discourse Analysis. *Review of Higher Education, 28*(4), 527–549. doi:10.1353/rhe.2005.0033.

Bailey, T. R. (2002). Community Colleges in the 21st Century: Challenges and Opportunities. In P. A. Graham & N. Stacey (Eds.), *The knowledge Economy and Postsecondary Education* (pp. 59–76). Washington, DC: National Academies Press.

Bailey, T. (2009). Challenge and Opportunity: Rethinking the Role and Function of Developmental Education in Community College. *New Directions for Community Colleges* (No. 145), 11–30. doi: 10.1002/cc.352.

Bailey, T., Badway, N., & Gumport, P. J. (2001). *For-Profit Higher Education and Community Colleges*. Stanford, CA: National Center for Postsecondary Improvement.

Bailey, T. R., Jaggars, S. S., & Jenkins, D. (2015). *Redesigning America's Community Colleges: A Clearer Path to Student Success*. Cambridge, MA: Harvard University Press.

Bailey, T., & Morest, V. S. (Eds.). (2006). *Defending the Community College Equity Agenda*. Baltimore, MD: Johns Hopkins University Press.

Barr, R. B., & Tagg, J. (1995, November/December) From Teaching to Learning: A New Paradigm for Undergraduate Education. *Change, 27*(6), 13–25.

Beach, J. M. (2011). *Gateway to Opportunity: A History of the Community College in the United States*. Herndon, VA : Stylus.

Boggs, G. R. (1991). *Palomar College 2005: A Shared Vision*. Unpublished document.

Boggs, G. R. (1993). Reinventing Community Colleges. *Community College Journal, 64*(3), 4–5.

Boggs, G. R. (1996). The Learning Paradigm. *Community College Journal, 66*(3), 24–27.

Boggs, G. R. (2006). *Handbook on Ceo–Board Relations and Responsibilities*. Washington, DC: Rowan & Littlefield.

Boggs, G. R. (2011) Community Colleges in the Spotlight and Community Colleges in the Spotlight and Under the Microscope. *New Directions for Community Colleges, 2011*(156), 3–22.

Boylan, H. (1999). Harvard Symposium 2000: Developmental education demographics, outcomes. *Journal of Developmental Education, 23*(2), 2–4, 6, 8.

Boyland, H. R. (1999). Exploring Alternatives to Remediation. *Journal of Developmental Education, 22*(3), 2–8.

Brint, S., & Karabel, J. (1991). *The Diverted Dream: Community Colleges and the Promise of Educational Opportunity in America, 1900–1985*. New York, NY: Oxford University Press.

Bryson, J. M. (2004). *Strategic Planning for Public and Nonprofit Organizations* (3rd ed.). San Francisco, CA: Jossey-Bass.

Bryson, J. M., & Alston, F. K. (2005). *Creating and Implementing Your Strategic Plan* (2nd ed.). San Francisco, CA: Jossey-Bass.

Calderon, A., & Mathies, C. (2013). Institutional Research in the Future: Challenges within Higher Education and the Need for Excellence in Professional Practice. *New Directions for Institutional Research* (No. 157), 77–90.

Center for Community College Student Engagement. (2012). *A Matter of Degrees: Promising Practices for Community College Student Success (A First Look)*. Austin: University of Texas at Austin, Community College Leadership Program. Retrieved from: http://www.cccse.org.

Center for Research on Learning and Teaching. (2009). *Multicultural Teaching: Information and Strategies*. Retrieved from: http://www.crlt.umich.edu/tstrategies/tsmdt.php.

Cohen, A. M., & Brawer, F. B. (2008). *The American Community College* (5th ed.) San Francisco, CA: Jossey-Bass.

College Rewired. (2012). Lumina Foundation Focus. Lumina Foundation (Summer 2012). Retrieved from: http://www.luminafoundation.org.

Coman, A., & Ronen, B. (2009). Focused SWOT: Diagnosing Critical Strengths and Weaknesses. *International Journal of Production Research, 40*(20), 5677–5689.

Complete College America. (2012). Remediation: Higher Education's Bridge to Nowhere 2012. Retrieved from: www.completecollege.org.

Davies, T. G. (1999). *Transfer Student Experiences: Comparing Their Academic and Social Lives at the Community College and University*. Retrieved from: http://www-vis.lbl.gov/~romano/Ed198-SEM/TransferStudentExperiences.pdf.

DeSantis, N. (2013, June 26). Early-College High Schools Benefit Students, Study Finds. *The Chronicle of Higher Education*. Retrieved from http://chronicle.com/blogs/ticker/early-college-high-schools-benefit-students-study-finds/62289.

Dougherty, K. J. (1994). *The Contradictory College: The Conflict Origins, Impacts, and Futures of the Community College*. SUNY Series in Frontiers in Education. Albany: State University of New York Press.

Dougherty, K. J., & Townsend, B. K. (2006). Community College Missions: A Theoretical and Historical Perspective. *New Directions for Community Colleges, 2006*, 5–13. doi: 10.1002/cc.254.

EDUCAUSE. EDUCAUSE Review 50, no. 1 (January/February 2015). Retrieved from http://er.educause.edu/articles/2015/1/educause-review-print-edition-volume-50-number-1-januaryfebruary-2015.

Erpenbach, W. J., & Forte, E. (2007). *Statewide Educational Accountability Systems Under the NCLB Act: A Report on 2007 Amendments to State Plans*. Washington, DC: Council of Chief State School Officers.

Fain, P. (2016, February 8). Low Income, High Graduation Rate. *Inside Higher Ed.* Retrieved from https://www.insidehighered.com/news/2016/02/08/programs-have-success-helping-low-income-students-graduate.

Floyd, D. L., Haley, A., Eddy, P. L., & Antczak, L. (2009). Celebrating the Past, Creating the Future: 50 Years of Community College Research. *Community College Journal of Research and Practice, 33,* 216–237.

Floyd, D. L., & Walker, K.P. (2008) The Community College Baccalaureate: Putting the Pieces Together. *Community College Journal of Research and Practice, 33*(20), 90–124.

Gonzalez, J. (2010, October 10). Obama Praises Community Colleges Amid Doubts About His Commitment. *Chronicle of Higher Education.* Retrieved from: http://chronicle.com/article/Obama-Praises-Community/124869/.

Green. D. (2006). Historically Underserved Students: What We Know, What We Still Need to Know. *New Directions for Community Colleges, 2006*(135), 21–28.

Gross, D. B. (1999). Diversity and Complexity in the Classroom: Considerations of Race, Ethnicity, and Gender. *Tools for Teaching.* Retrieved from: http://honolulu.hawaii.edu/intranet/committees/FacDevCom/guidebk/teachtip/diverse.htm.

Handel, S. J. (2009). Transfer and Part-Time Student: The Gulf Separating Community Colleges and Selective Universities. *Change, 41*(4), 48–53.

Harris, Z. M., & Kayes, P. (April, 1995). Multicultural and International Challenges to the Community College: A Model for College-Wide Proactive Response. Paper presented at Annual Convention of the American Association of Community Colleges, Minneapolis, MN. (ED 387 173).

Heaton, P. (2015). *Opportunity Knocking: How Community College Presidents Can Lead a New Era of Advancement.* Washington, DC: CASE.

Horn, L., Nevill, S., & Griffith, J. (2006). *Profiles of Undergraduates in U.S. Postsecondary Education Institutions, 2003–2004: With a Special Analysis of Community College Students.* Washington, DC: US Department of Education, National Center for Education Statistics.

Jacobs, J. (2000). What Is the Future for Postsecondary Vocational Education? *Update on research and leadership, 12*(1), 1–4.

Jacobs, J., & Dougherty, K. J. (2006). The Uncertain Future of the Community College Workforce Development Mission. In B .K. Townsend & K. J. Dougherty (Eds.), *Community College Missions in the 21st Century* (pp. 53–62). San Francisco, CA: Jossey-Bass.

Jenkins, D. (2014). Overview of the Guided Pathways Approach. Community College Research Center Teachers College, Columbia University. Unpublished paper.

Jenkins, D., & Cho, S. W. (2014). *Get With the Program . . . and Finish It: Building Guided Pathways to Accelerate Student Completion* (CCRC Working Paper No. 66). Retrieved from http://ccrc.tc.columbia.edu/media/ k2/attachments/get-with-the-program-and-finish-it-2.pdf.

Heaton, P. (2015). *Opportunity Knocking: How Community College Presidents Can Lead a New Era of Advancement.* Washington, DC: CASE.

Keyton, J. N. (2011). *Communication and Organizational Culture: A Key to Understanding Work Experience.* (2nd ed.). London: Sage.

Lanty, M., Hussar, W., Snyder, T., Kena, G., Kewal Ramani, A., Kemp, J., Bianco, K., Dinkes, R. (2009). *The Condition of Education 2009* (NCES 2009-081). Washington, DC: National Center for Education Statistics, Institute of Education Sciences, U.S. Department of Education.

Levine, J. (2000). The Revised Institution: The Community College Mission at the End of the Twentieth Century. *Community College Review, 28*(2), 1–24.

Levine, J. (2004). The Community College as a Baccalaureate-Granting Institution. *Review of Higher Education, 28*(1), 1–22.

Levinson, D. L. (2005). The Growth of Community Colleges in the Twentieth Century. *Community Colleges* (pp. 43–73). Santa Barbara, CA: ABC-CLIO.

Lieberman, J. E. (1985), Combining High School and College: LaGuardia's Middle College High School. *New Directions for Teaching and Learning* (No. 24). 47–57. doi: 10.1002/tl.37219852407.

Linn, R. L. (2004). Accountability Models. In S. H. Fuhrman & R. F. Elmore (Eds.), *Redesigning Accountability Systems for Education* (pp. 73–95). New York, NY: Teachers College Press.

Lorenzo, A. L., & LeCroy, N. A. (1994). *A Framework for Fundamental Change in the Community College: Creating a Culture of Responsiveness.* Warren, MI: Macomb Community College Institute for Future Studies. (ED 369 432)

College Rewired. (2012). Lumina Foundation Focus. Lumina Foundation (Summer 2012). Retrieved from: http://www.luminafoundation.org.

Mars, M. M., & Ginter, M. (2007). Connecting Organizational Environments with the Instructional Technology Practices of Community College Faculty. *Community College Review, 34*(4), 324–343.

McPhail, C. J. (2004, October 29). Staying Focused on Suitable Missions. *Chronicle of Higher Education.* Retrieved from http://www.accbd.org/ articles/index.php/attachments/single/35.

McPhail, C. J., & McPhail, I. P. (2006). Prioritizing Community College Missions: A Directional Effort. *New Directions for Community Colleges* (No.136), 91–99. doi: 10.1002/cc.263

MDRC. (2013). *Developmental Education: A Barrier to a Postsecondary Credential for Millions of Americans*. Retrieved from http://www.mdrc.org/publication/developmental-education-barrier-postsecondary-credential-millions-americans.

Middle College National Consortium: Expanding College Access. (n.d.). Retrieved from http://mcnc.us.

Moorcroft, D. (2003). Linking communication strategy with organizational goals. *Strategic Communication Management, 7, 6.*

National Center for Education Statistics. (2004). *The Condition of Education 2004* (NCES 2004-077). Washington DC: U.S. Government Printing Office.

O'Banion, T. (1997). *A Learning College for the 21st Century*. Phoenix, AZ: American Council on Education and the Oryx Press.

Parry, M., Field, K., & Supiano, B. (2014, July 14). The Gates Effect. *Chronicle of Higher Education*. Retrieved from: http://chronicle.com/article/The-Gates-Effect/140323/?cid=at.

Phillippe, K. A., & Sullivan, L. G. (2005). *National Profile of Community Colleges: Trends and Statistics*. Washington, DC: Community College Press.

Pincus, F. (1980). The False Promises of Community College: Class Conflict and Vocational Education. *Harvard Educational Review, 50*(30), 332–361.

Quigley, M., & Bailey, T. (2003). *Community College Movement in Perspective: Teachers College Responds to the Truman Commission*. Oxford, MA: Scarecrow Press.

Reed, M. (2013, June 26). A Warning to My Colleagues. *Inside Higher Ed*. Retrieved from https://www.insidehighered.com/blogs/confessions-community-college-dean/warning-my-colleagues.

Rhoades, R. A. & Valadez, R. (1996). *Democracy, Multiculturalism, and the Community College: A Critical Perspective*. New York, NY: Taylor & Francis.

Rothaermel, F. T. (2012). *Strategic Management: Concepts and Cases*. New York, NY: McGraw-Hill/Irwin.

Roueche, J. E., & Jones, B. R. (2005). *The Entrepreneurial Community College*. Washington, DC: American Association of Community Colleges.

Shannon, H. D., & Smith, R. C. (2006). A Case for the Community College's Open Access Mission. *New Directions for Community Colleges, 2006,* 15–21. doi: 10.1002/cc.255.

Shipley, D. (1995, October). Transforming Community Colleges Using a Learning Outcomes Approach. Paper presented at a workshop sponsored by the Advanced Education Council of British Columbia and the Centre for Curriculum and Professional Development, Richmond, British Columbia, Canada. (ED 388 346)

Stewart, D. P. (2008). Technology as a Management Tool in the Community College Classroom: Challenges and Benefits. *MERLOT Journal of Online Learning and Teaching, 4*(4), 459–468.

Szelényi, K., & Chang, J. C. (2002). Educating Immigrants: A Community College Role. *Community College Review, 32,* 55–73.

Terryll-Powell, Y & Barnett, B. (Eds.). (2003). *Course 10: Integrating Cultural Diversity Into the Curriculum.* Retrieved from: http://www.wa-skills.com/PDFs/10divtext.pdf.

Tillery, D., & Deegan, W. (1985). The evolution of two-year colleges through four generations. In D. Tillery & W. Deegan (Eds.), *Renewing the American Community College* (pp. 3–33). San Francisco, CA: Jossey-Bass.

Truman Commission on Higher Education. (1947). *Higher Education for Democracy: A Report of the President's Commission on Higher Education, Vol. 1, Establishing the Goals.* New York, NY: Harper & Brothers.

University of Kansas Work Group for Community Health and Development. (2010). Community Assessment, Agenda Setting, and Choice of Broad Strategies. *Community Tool Box.* Lawrence: Author. Retrieved from: http://ctb.ku.edu/en/tablecontents/index.aspx.

Vaughan, G. B. (2006). Critics of the Community College: An Overview. *New Directions for Community Colleges* (No. 32), 1–14. doi: 10.1002/cc.36819803203.

Watson, L. W., Williams, F. K., & Derby, D. C. (2005). Contemporary Multicultural Issues: Student, Faculty, and Administrator Perceptions. *Community College Enterprise, 11*(1), 79–92.

White House (2009, July 14). *Excerpts of the President's remarks in Warren, Michigan, and fact sheet on the American Graduation Initiative,* Office of the Press Secretary. Retrieved from https://www.whitehouse.gov/the-press-office/excerpts-presidents-remarks-warren-michigan-and-fact-sheet-american-graduation-init.

Zinshteyn, M. (2015, August 30). *For-Profit Universities.* Education Writer's Association. Retrieved from: http://www.ewa.org/profit-universities.

3

ACCOUNTABILITY, SCORECARDS, REGULATIONS, AND ACCREDITATION

Accountability

The Commission on the Future of Higher Education, convened by US Secretary of Education Margaret Spellings in 2005, and its subsequent report, *A TEST OF LEADERSHIP: Charting the Future of U.S. Higher Education* (Miller et al., 2006), initiated a renewed focus on accountability in higher education. Although a primary motivation of the secretary and her commission was to provide consumer information in more transparent and understandable formats to prospective students and parents, there was also a growing concern about rapidly increasing tuition costs, rising student indebtedness, and quality concerns from business leaders about the workforce readiness of college and university graduates. Although many of the recommendations of the Spellings Commission were not implemented, the report, nonetheless, has had a lasting impact on higher education transparency and accountability. Higher education associations, including the American Association of Community Colleges (AACC), concerned that government officials might develop accountability measures that were inappropriate and overly burdensome, began to develop their own voluntary systems and frameworks.

The end of President George W. Bush's administration did not diminish the federal interest in the performance of higher education. If anything, the administration of President Barack Obama increased the focus on accountability through regulation and proposed a college and university rating system (US Department of Education, 2014). Although federal policy makers have been most concerned about alleged abuses and student loan defaults in the for-profit sector, regulations and potential rating systems also affect other segments of higher education, including public community colleges.

The federal interest in accountability is fueled by its annual investment of more than $169 billion in student financial assistance to more than 15 million students (Baum & Payea, 2013, p. 10). Policy makers, reflecting *cost* *debt* public anxiety, are also becoming more concerned about the rising cost of college tuition and how much students have to borrow to pay for it. *Forbes* reported that in 2013, student indebtedness had reached $1.2 trillion (Denhart, 2013). The Institute for College Access and Success (TICAS) reported that in 2013, 69 percent of graduating seniors at public and private nonprofit colleges had federal and private student loans *69%* averaging $28,000 (TICAS, 2014). In addition, the student loan default rate of about 14 percent (Stratford & Fain, 2014) within the first three years after graduation is a significant burden on taxpayers. In too many instances, graduates cannot get jobs with salaries sufficient to pay off their student loans.

The US Department of Education has few tools at its disposal to hold higher education institutions accountable for maintaining quality and controlling costs. That is why we have seen increased pressure on accreditors, efforts to encourage stronger state oversight, regulations governing gainful employment after graduation, and a proposed rating system. Each of these efforts, however, has unintended negative consequences. State authorization, for example, sets up a costly bureaucratic requirement for colleges that enroll online students who reside in states other than where the college is physically located. Gainful employment and loan default regulations hold institutions accountable for situations that may not be in their control, such as the economy, unemployment rates, or the financial responsibility of the graduates. A national rating system does not make a lot of sense for community colleges with their diverse missions and local community focus.

States, pushed by the federal government and, in some cases, by organizations such as Complete College America, have also become more interested in accountability—with a particular focus on college completion and the effectiveness of remediation. States have begun to publish scorecards showing completion data for colleges. Although performance-based funding has raised concerns about the potentials for limiting access for the most at-risk students and lowering standards—and some research studies have shown little impact—states are increasingly moving to systems of funding based upon outcome measures in addition to enrollment. Hillman, Tandberg, and Fryar (2015) found that performance-based funding has had little immediate effect on retention rates or associate degree productivity. However, they found that community colleges produced more short-term certificates after the policy reform.

In November 2015, the Lumina Foundation began to release policy papers on performance-based funding in higher education (Weathers, 2015). The foundation noted that at least thirty-five states are either developing or using funding formulas that link support for public colleges to student completion rates, degree production numbers, or other metrics. The Lumina papers look at how those policies are working, with particular interest in their impact on the completion rates of underserved student populations. The foundation believes that the need for finance systems oriented around improving student outcomes is urgent, especially for ensuring more equitable outcomes for students from all racial and ethnic backgrounds. We recommend that community college leaders become involved in the policy discussions in their states so that the performance metrics make sense for the colleges and their students.

In 2008, the American Association of Community Colleges, the Association of Community College Trustees, and the College Board initiated a Lumina Foundation–funded effort to develop a national Voluntary Framework of Accountability (VFA) for community colleges. Community colleges needed a process through which they could communicate data that paint a more accurate portrait of the sector and its unique role in American higher education. Lack of commonly accepted performance measures for community colleges has often led to a misunderstanding of the institutions and an underestimation of their effectiveness and the contributions they make.

Certainly, the multiple missions of community colleges complicate how institutional performance is measured. Students enter a community college for myriad reasons. Some enroll to prepare for careers; others attend for a single course to upgrade specific job skills, perhaps to earn promotions; and others seek baccalaureate degrees by completing their lower-division courses at a community college and transfer to a four-year college or university. Still others enter community colleges for personal enrichment alone. The varied needs and individual goals of community college students, which represent appropriate and vital aspects of the community college mission, are difficult to measure in meaningful ways.

Current methodologies measuring higher education productivity do not capture well the work of community colleges or the students who attend them. The federal higher education methodology, The Integrated Postsecondary Education Data System (IPEDS), for example, is focused on measuring the amount of time it takes for a student to complete a degree or certificate. Although this represents an important dimension of productivity, it describes little of what is actually going on at community colleges. There are at least three reasons for this.

1. Only first-time, full-time, degree-seeking students are currently included in the IPEDS calculation for time to degree, and 62 percent of community college students are enrolled part-time.

2. Success is commonly defined as the completion of a degree or certificate, yet the educational goals of community college students vary widely, often in ways both richer and more idiosyncratic than traditional academic measures of completion.

3. Even in those instances in which two- and four-year institutional goals overlap, community colleges do not receive credit for the work they do. A case in point is transfer. Although community colleges prepare thousands of students for transfer to four-year institutions and the baccalaureate, the students who transfer from their institutions before attaining an associate degree are classified as "drop-outs." Transfer data are not usually systematically reported back to the community colleges, and community colleges are regularly and often unjustly criticized for having low transfer rates.

Systems of accountability that track only students who are first-time, full-time, degree-seeking freshmen at an institution do not make sense in an era when college students are more mobile than ever and in an environment in which most community college students attend part time. A few years ago, George Boggs met with a group of presidents of Historically Black Colleges and Universities and encouraged them to work with community colleges to increase the number of students who transfer to their institutions. The presidents responded that doing so could lower their measured student success rates because transfers are not first-time freshmen; the presidents were not willing to take that risk. Fortunately, officials in the US Department of Education are aware of this issue and are working to correct data systems.

Accountability systems have been employed by several states, local governments, accreditors, the federal government, researchers, and foundation-funded efforts such as the Achieving the Dream and Bridges to Opportunity projects. However, prior to VFA, there was no national accountability system designed specifically for community colleges.

Developing a community college accountability framework brought with it several challenges. For example, coordinating the multiple data-gathering efforts by states, accrediting agencies, and funded initiatives was a significant complication in developing the unified framework. Smaller community colleges often lack the resources and the expertise to collect and analyze data for participation in voluntary efforts on their own. Progress toward the implementation of the VFA on a larger scale can be followed on the AACC website.

In early 2015, three higher education associations unveiled an effort to take accountability a step further. The American Association of Community Colleges, the Association of Public and Land-grant Universities (APLU), and the American Association of State Colleges and Universities (AASCU) developed a partnership to measure outcomes of higher education postgraduation. The Post-Collegiate Outcomes Initiative, funded by the Bill & Melinda Gates Foundation, has developed a strategic framework to guide discussion of student outcomes after college—and measurement tools for reporting them. The framework and accompanying toolkit, shown on the AACC website at http://www.aacc.nche.edu/AboutCC/Trends/pco/Pages/default.aspx, are intended to broaden the conversation surrounding postcollegiate outcomes to include both economic and social capital contributions to both individuals and their communities (Fain, 2015).

The project's partners assembled subject-matter experts and institutional leaders to create a framework and application tools that will enable colleges and universities, policy makers, and the public to better understand and talk about postcollegiate outcomes in areas such as economic well-being, ongoing personal development, and social and civic engagement.

Scorecards

Although the federal proposal to rate colleges was controversial and was not implemented, some states are pushing ahead with scorecards that are intended to provide college information in a transparent fashion. One good example is the Student Success Scorecard developed by the California Community Colleges. The scorecard provides both statewide and individual college data on student profile, momentum points, and completion by student gender, age, ethnicity, and whether the student was prepared or underprepared for college. Momentum points include progression from remedial into college-level courses and progression at two different credit accumulation points. Information is also provided on completion to degree or transfer for the same student groupings. Persistence of students in career and technical education programs is also shown. Although the data are public and available from the California

Community College Chancellor's Office website (http://datamart.cccco. edu/Outcomes/Student_Success_Scorecard.aspx) they are more likely targeted toward institutional improvement than consumer information because students are unlikely to shop around for the community college they want to attend based upon the scorecard.

Regulations

Higher education institutions in the United States must comply with regulations that are imposed as a result of legislation, executive action, or court decisions. At the federal level, regulations are usually developed after the passage of a law by a process called "negotiated rulemaking," abbreviated Neg Reg. The US Department of Education and other federal agencies convene negotiations between representatives of the federal agency and representatives of affected groups. If the group is unsuccessful in coming to consensus on the language of a rule, the agency can develop its own language. In either case, the agency publishes the proposed rule in the *Federal Register* and then solicits public comments that are evaluated for inclusion in the final rule.

One of the most controversial federal regulations—and one that was not arrived at by consensus—is called "Gainful Employment." Through this regulation, the department hopes to ensure that students are graduating from reputable institutions and then are able to become employed, earning enough income to repay student loans. Although community colleges have criticized the Gainful Employment rules as being too burdensome, especially for institutions in which a small percentage of students borrow, for-profit colleges and their allies have consistently expressed the major concerns. Although the Association of Private Sector Colleges and Universities (APSCU) was successful in court in the past, its most recent suit against the US Department of Education to stop the Gainful Employment regulations from taking effect (Devaney, 2014) was not successful (Stratford, 2015). However, the association has promised to take its case to Congress.

The election of 2014 brought a majority of Republicans to both houses of Congress. Although Republicans traditionally have been stingier in providing funding to higher education, they have also been advocates for reduced regulation. Republican leaders have already pledged to reduce the regulatory burden on higher education, and they spoke out against the Obama administration's proposed rating system. They have also been more supportive of for-profit education, which has been a particular target for regulation by the Obama administration.

The US Department of Education requires colleges and universities to keep three-year cohort loan default rates below a specified percentage to avoid incurring a penalty that could eventually result in loss of institutional eligibility to administer federal financial aid to its students (Chitty, 2010). Because of their efforts to retain financial aid eligibility for their students, some community college leaders have refused to participate in federal loan programs. This decision has subjected them to criticism (Stratford, 2014). Some student advocates point out that this decision by college officials closes the door to less expensive borrowing for needy students and forces many of them to borrow from more expensive private lenders. However, college officials say they do not want to jeopardize their ability to offer Pell Grants to qualifying students because of a default rate that is not completely within their control. If colleges participate in the federal loan program, they do not have any discretion over the amount borrowed or the timing of the loan—nor whether the students are responsible enough to make the payments.

Another federal regulation that is often seen as burdensome is called "Return of Title IV." If a student who is receiving federal financial aid withdraws from college before completing 60 percent of the term, the federal government holds the institution responsible for returning a calculated share of Title IV funds that were disbursed to the student. The Return of Title IV regulation can create a significant staffing and financial burden on colleges.

Some regulations are the direct result of federal or state law. One example is the Clery Act, which requires colleges and universities to disclose information about crime on and around their campuses. The law is tied to an institution's participation in federal student financial aid programs, and it applies to most institutions of higher education, both public and private. The Clery Act, like the other regulations mentioned here, is enforced by the US Department of Education.

Another example of a regulation that is the direct result of federal legislation is Title IX of the Education Amendments of 1972, which protects people from discrimination based on gender in any institution that receives federal funding or whose students receive federal financial aid. Examples of the types of discrimination that are prohibited by Title IX include sexual harassment, the failure to provide equal opportunity in athletics, and discrimination based on pregnancy. To enforce Title IX, the US Department of Education maintains an Office for Civil Rights, with headquarters in Washington, D.C., and twelve regional offices across the United States. One of the most significant impacts of Title IX has been the growth of college athletic programs for women. Both the Clery Act and

Title IX are discussed in more detail in chapter 8 as they apply to campus safety and security.

Despite the best intentions of legislators, government regulations can force the focus of institutions away from the mission of student learning. In California, for example, legislation requires community colleges to spend at least 50 percent of their revenue on classroom faculty. Librarians, counselors, student advisors, and financial aid officers are "on the other side of the Fifty Percent Law" (Santa Clarita Community College District, 2009). The ratio of student advisors or counselors is most often greater than a thousand to one. Research clearly demonstrates that investments in student guidance pay off in accelerated and increased student learning and success (Jenkins & Cho, 2012). Despite the fact that community college students are the most financially disadvantaged students in higher education, they are less likely to receive the financial aid they deserve (JBL Associates, 2010). Yet the Fifty Percent Law severely limits what local college faculty and academic administrators can do on their campuses to meet the needs of students in these areas. As it has turned out, this law is a barrier to increasing student learning and success. Perhaps state legislators and the faculty unions that lobby them do not trust local trustees and administrators to spend resources appropriately, but this law, in its current form, detracts from the mission of student learning.

Another example of state regulation that is not focused on institutional mission is the result of legislation mandating that individuals be allowed to carry guns on campus. The American Association of State Colleges and Universities (Hurley, Harnish, & Parker, 2015) predicts that legislation to impose this kind of state mandate will continue to be introduced. The number of states in which lawmakers have stripped institutions' ability to ban guns on campus at the end of 2015 stands at seven. At the beginning of 2016, twenty states prohibited concealed weapons on campus, while twenty-three states allowed individual public institutions to set their own concealed weapons policy. The higher education and law enforcement community, in unison with overwhelming public opinion, do not support the policy of arming civilians on college campuses, which are among the safest sanctuaries in American society. However, pro-gun organizations believe that allowing guns on campus will deter crime by creating an environment in which criminals and terrorists will be less secure to carry out acts of gun violence.

Because of criticism of how colleges and universities deal with sexual assault charges, new federal and state laws may soon require institutions to follow specific procedures and to file reports with law enforcement agencies and federal and state agencies when a charge is filed.

Accreditation

The US peer-controlled systems to assure educational quality and encourage improvement are unique in a world in which most countries rely on direct government oversight. Two distinct types of US higher education accreditation are specialized or program accreditation and institutional accreditation. Some programs, such as nursing, business, and engineering have developed their own accreditation programs to ensure minimum standards of quality from one institution to the next. Specialized accreditation is voluntary, but many institutions use their specialized accreditation status to promote their programs to prospective students, other higher education institutions, and employers.

Some institutional accreditors are national in scope and generally accredit institutions with a special curricular focus. Examples include faith-based, career-based, and distance education accreditors. However, the type of institutional accreditation that is most sought after in the United States is regional. All US public higher education institutions and several proprietary institutions have chosen to be regionally accredited. There are seven regional accreditors located in six regions in the United States: New England Association of Schools and Colleges (NEASC), Middle States Association of Colleges and Schools (MSACS), the Higher Learning Commission (HLC), Northwest Commission on Colleges and Universities (NWCCU), the Southern Association of Colleges and Schools (SACS), and the Western Association of Schools and Colleges (WASC)— which is divided into a commission for senior colleges and the Accrediting Commission for Community and Junior Colleges (ACCJC).

Because of the US government's reliance on institutional accreditation to assure quality in an environment that is often politically charged, the system often comes under attack. On the one hand, critics say that the current system is designed to protect the status quo and is hostile to innovation. On the other hand, accreditors are criticized for allowing institutions with poor outcomes or poor financial oversight to remain open. Policy makers question why more colleges are not being forced to close— unless, of course, it is a college in their voting district.

Perhaps the most serious challenge to an accrediting agency by representatives of its member institutions occurred in 2015. A task force appointed by California Community College Chancellor Brice W. Harris concluded in a report released in August 2015 that the ACCJC had lost the confidence of the colleges, noting disproportionately high and frequent sanctions imposed on California colleges when compared to colleges in other regions of the country. In November 2015, the California

Community Colleges Board of Governors unanimously directed the state Chancellor's Office to develop a new model for accrediting the system's colleges and to report back in March 2016 on details and a timeline for implementing the changes. The board approved the resolution citing the need to raise the professionalism of accreditation in California, stating that the Accrediting Commission for Community and Junior Colleges, which also accredits institutions in Hawaii and the Pacific Islands, had lost credibility with its peers and no longer met the current and anticipated needs of California community colleges.

The board also cited the community college system's establishment of bachelor's degree programs and its strengthened transfer pathways, such as the Associate Degree for Transfer program, as impetus for peer review from four-year colleges and universities to ensure top quality for students. ACCJC does not accredit four-year institutions, although it had been cooperating with the WASC Senior College and University Commission to accredit community colleges in the Pacific Islands that offer a limited number of baccalaureates. The US Department of Education terminated the agreement that allowed the two commissions to accredit community colleges that offer baccalaureates, leaving an accreditation void at a time when several California community colleges are planning to offer baccalaureate programs.

The outcome of the challenge to ACCJC is not clear. One conceivable outcome would be the merger of ACCJC and the WASC Senior College and University Commission, which would bring the western region into compliance with the other five regional commissions. However, the process would be complex and would involve approval of the member colleges and the US Department of Education as well as the willingness of the WASC Senior College and University Commission to accept all of the members of ACCJC.

The accreditors themselves undergo an accreditation of sorts by the US Department of Education. The National Advisory Committee on Institutional Quality and Integrity (NACIQI) advises the Secretary of Education on matters related to higher education accreditation and the eligibility of higher education institutions to participate in the federal student aid programs. Its primary function is to provide recommendations to the secretary concerning whether the standards of an accreditor are sufficiently rigorous and effective in their application to ensure that the accreditor is reliable in certifying the quality of the education and training provided by the institutions or programs it accredits. Accrediting agencies must provide evidence of compliance with all the criteria for recognition. When the Secretary of Education recognizes an accreditor, the institutions it accredits are eligible to participate in the federal student aid programs, providing they meet appropriate federal regulations.

Accreditors can also choose to be recognized by the Council for Higher Education Accreditation (CHEA), a national advocate and institutional voice for self-regulation of academic quality through accreditation. CHEA, based in Washington, D.C., is an association of three thousand degree-granting colleges and universities that recognizes sixty institutional and programmatic accrediting organizations. CHEA is also a national voice for accreditation and quality assurance to the US Congress and US Department of Education. CHEA is the only nongovernmental higher education organization in the United States that verifies the rigor of accrediting agencies. Recognition by CHEA affirms that the standards and processes of the accrediting organization are consistent with the CHEA-established academic quality, improvement, and accountability expectations. Information about CHEA, its standards, and the institutional members can be found on its website (http://www.chea.org).

The seven regional accrediting commissions have developed an informal coordinating group, called the Council of Regional Accreditation Commissions (C-RAC). Through C-RAC, the commissions have advocated with policy makers to defend accreditation and have developed common accreditation guides and principles of good practice. The C-RAC members communicate regularly as they address common issues.

Institutional accreditation commonly requires a period of self-study— resulting in a self-study report and a visit by a team of peers from other higher education institutions to validate the self-study and to identify any areas in which the institution is not in compliance with accreditation standards. The visiting team then prepares an accreditation report, which is submitted to the accreditation commission with a copy to the institution. The report usually highlights institutional commendations and also makes recommendations for improvement. If the institution is believed to be out of compliance with accreditation standards, it is noted in the report. The commission then decides the accreditation status of the institution. If the institution is in need of improvement, the commission might issue a sanction, which could include a warning or probation. This type of action usually requires the institution to submit an interim report on corrective action and may require an additional peer visit. The most serious sanction is called "show cause," which essentially is the institution's last chance to show why its accreditation (and thus its federal financial aid eligibility) should not be revoked. Loss of accredited status means closure of the institution. Although visits are periodic, institutions are expected to be in compliance with accreditation standards at all times.

From October 2009, when data were first consistently collected, through March 2014, the US Government Accountability Office (GAO) found that accreditors issued at least 984 sanctions to 621 schools, terminating the accreditation of 66 schools (GAO, 2014). GAO found that accreditors most commonly cited financial rather than academic problems. The GAO criticized the US Department of Education for not consistently using accreditor sanction information for oversight, as required by law (GAO, 2014). These types of GAO reports usually require a response from NACIQI and the Secretary of Education.

One of the most contested accreditation-related actions in recent history involves the City College of San Francisco (CCSF), one of the largest community colleges in the United States. ACCJC, the college's regional accreditor, found that the college had ignored previous warnings about its governance and financial condition. After a period of Show Cause, the commission acted to withdraw accreditation. The State Community College Board of Governors acted to replace the elected Board of Trustees at CCSF with a special trustee to steer the college back into accreditation status. After intense political pressure from members of Congress and a faculty union complaint sent to the US Department of Education, the commission developed a process for the college to have its accreditation reinstated. College leadership is focused almost entirely on the reinstatement process. The San Francisco city attorney sued ACCJC in an attempt to keep the college open. The result of the lawsuit was an injunction that permitted the college to demand a detailed written account of the accreditor's 2013 claims that the college fell short of accreditation standards in ten specific areas. Significantly, the court did not overrule the actions of the accrediting commission.

Issues to Consider

A. One of the recommendations of the Spellings Commission was to create a national Unit Record Data System so data could provide information on student pathways through education. Why did Congress specifically prohibit this recommendation? What would be the potential advantages and disadvantages of a national data system?

B. Some policy makers argue that tuition cost increases are the result of increases in student financial aid. Do you believe this is the case? If so, is it true for all institutions of higher education? What role does state disinvestment in subsidies to higher education play in tuition cost increases for public institutions?

C. Are federal Gainful Employment regulations an effective way to insure institutional integrity? Does the government have a right to ask that program graduates be employed at salaries that allow them to repay student loans? What problems could Gainful Employment rules create for colleges?

D. What issues are created by colleges in insuring that federal Title IX regulations are followed? How have the regulations affected college policies and programs?

E. Are the community college officials who choose not to participate in the federal student loan program in order to protect Pell eligibility correct in their action?

F. What is the rationale for a federal college and university rating system? What are the reasons for the objections to national ratings for US community colleges?

G. Did the Accrediting Commission for Community and Junior Colleges have sufficient reason to remove accreditation from the City College of San Francisco? Did the accreditor make any mistakes? What might be the wider effect of the court case against ACCJC?

H. Is the California Community College Board of Governors justified in its action to seek a new accreditor for California community colleges? What alternatives do the colleges have for regional accreditation?

I. Is the regional system of institutional accreditation an outdated model? Should there instead be a single national institutional accreditor with a single set of standards?

J. Should the Department of Education decouple accreditation from eligibility for federal financial aid and instead develop a system of federal quality assurance like that found in other countries?

Case Scenario

You receive a notification from your regional accreditor that high school teachers in dual-credit courses must have a master's degree in the specialties they're teaching, or they need at least eighteen graduate-level credit hours within their specialties. Your college has until September 2017 to assure that any high school teachers who teach college-level courses meet these requirements. Many of the high school teachers teaching dual enrollment courses may either have just a bachelor's degree or a master's degree in education but not in the subject matter they're teaching. What issues does the scenario create? What leadership competencies are involved? Who should be involved in addressing the situation? What actions would you take? Are there lessons to be learned?

REFERENCES

Baum, S., & Payea, K. (2013). *Trends in Student Aid 2013*. The College Board. Retrieved from http://trends.collegeboard.org/sites/default/files/student-aid-2013-full-report.pdf.

Chitty, H. (2010). A New Formula for Cohort Default Rates. *University Business*. Retrieved from http://www.universitybusiness.com/article/new-formula-cohort-default-rates.

Denhart, C. (2013, August 7). How the $1.2 Trillion College Debt Crisis Is Crippling Students, Parents and the Economy. *Forbes*. Retrieved from http://www.forbes.com/sites/specialfeatures/2013/08/07/how-the-college-debt-is-crippling-students-parents-and-the-economy/.

Devaney, T. (2014). Colleges Sue Feds Over "Gainful Employment" Rule. *The Hill*. Retrieved from http://thehill.com/regulation/court-battles/223218-private-schools-challenge-unlawful-college-rules-in-court.

Fain, P. (2015, January 9). Measuring Substance. *Inside Higher Ed*. Retrieved from https://www.insidehighered.com/news/2015/01/09/associations-weigh-how-gauge-post-college-outcomes.

Government Accountability Office. (2014). *Higher Education: Education Should Strengthen Oversight of Schools and Accreditors* (GAO-15–59). Retrieved from http://www.gao.gov/products/GAO-15–59.

Hillman, N., Tandberg, D., & Fryar, A. (2015). *Evaluating the Impacts of "New" Performance Funding in Higher Education*. American Education Research Association. Retrieved from http://www.aera.net/Newsroom/RecentAERAResearch/EvaluatingtheImpactsof"New"PerformanceFundinginHigherEducation/tabid/15792/Default.aspx.

Hurley, D., Harnish, T., & Parker, E. (2015). *Top 10 State Policy Higher Education Issues for 2105*. Washington, DC: American Association of State Colleges and Universities. Retrieved from http://www.aascu.org/policy/publications/policy-matters/Top10StatePolicyIssues2015.pdf.

JBL Associates. (2010). *The Financial Aid Challenge*. New York, NY: College Board. Retrieved from http://www.aacc.nche.edu/Advocacy/Documents/10b_1790_FAFSA_Exec_Report_WEB_100517.pdf.

Jenkins, D., & Cho, S-W. (2012). *Get With the Program: Accelerating Community College Students' Entry Into and Completion of Programs of Study*. New York, NY: Columbia University, Teachers College, Community College Research Center. Retrieved from http://www.wsac.wa.gov/sites/default/files/2014.ptw.(26).pdf.

Miller, C., et al. (2006). *A TEST OF LEADERSHIP: Charting the Course of U.S. Higher Education*. Washington, DC: US Department of Education.

Retrieved from https://www2.ed.gov/about/bdscomm/list/hiedfuture/
reports/pre-pub-report.pdf.

Santa Clarita Community College District. (2009, December 1). *The Fifty
Percent Law Requirements*. Retrieved from http://www.acbo.org/files/
Spring%20Conference/05-16-11%20Fifty%20Percent%20Law%
20Summary%20for%20ACBO.pdf.

Stratford, M. (2014, July 15). Inequitable Access to Loans. *Inside Higher Ed*.
Retrieved from https://www.insidehighered.com/news/2014/07/15/report-
minority-community-college-students-denied-access-federal-loans.

Stratford, M. (2015, May 28). Judge Upholds "Gainful" Rule. *Inside Higher Ed*.
Retrieved from https://www.insidehighered.com/news/2015/05/28/federal-
judge-tosses-profit-colleges'-challenge-'gainful-employment'-rule.

Stratford, M., & Fain, P. (2014). Default Rates Dip (Slightly). *Inside Higher Ed*.
Retrieved from https://www.insidehighered.com/news/2014/09/25/default-
rate-federal-loans-ticks-down-slightly-21-colleges-face-sanctions-
high-rates.

Student Success Scorecard. *California Community Colleges*. Retrieved from
http://scorecard.cccco.edu/scorecardrates.aspx?CollegeID=000#home.

The Institute for College Access and Success. (2014). *Student Debt and the Class
of 2013*. Oakland, CA,: Author. Retrieved from http://projectonstudentdebt.
org/files/pub/classof2013.pdf.

US Department of Education. (2014). *For Public Feedback: A College Rating
Framework*. Washington, DC: Author. Retrieved from https://www.
insidehighered.com/sites/default/server_files/files/ratings%20framework%
20draft.pdf.

Weathers, L. (2015). Lumina Foundation Papers. Retrieved from https://www.
luminafoundation.org/news-and-events/s7-outcomes-based-funding-
paper-series.

4

FINANCE, COST, AND
THE ECONOMY

Economic Benefits of Higher Education

Numerous studies have shown the significant and positive benefits of postsecondary education to an individual (Baum, Ma, & Payea, 2013). In general, the more education that people have, the greater will be their lifetime earnings and quality of life. However, society as a whole also enjoys a significant financial return on public investment in higher education. With higher levels of education come greater earnings, lower unemployment, increased tax revenues, and decreased dependence on social welfare and safety nets. Factors such as these yield tremendous economic returns on public investment in higher education. Between increases in tax revenues and decreases in government expenditures such as unemployment benefits and incarceration, the taxpayer benefit over a lifetime for having a student complete postsecondary education compared to high school ranges from $24,000 to $51,000, depending on race and gender (Mullin, 2011). One study found that the return on investment to state and local governments from providing funds to community colleges averaged 16.1 percent nationally in 2007 (Economic Modeling Specialists, International, 2007). Mullin (2011) makes the point that the return to communities on public investment in community colleges is enhanced by their local focus. Community college students are more likely to remain in their communities after completing their educational programs. Community colleges provide these benefits to society much less expensively to both the student and the public than any other form of public higher education.

Effect of Economic Cycles

Even though it is well documented that public investment in higher education pays off, state support to higher education is one of the first items to be cut during economic downturns; and because of their significant dependence on public support, funding for community colleges is usually cut the most. Instability and uncertainty in funding create significant issues for community college leaders, especially because student enrollments are countercyclical with the economy: when the economy enters a period of decline, student enrollment pressure increases while state funding usually decreases; when the economy recovers, enrollments decline, and state funding is often slow to recover. Each of these points in an economic cycle brings challenges and issues for leaders. Understanding economic issues and preparing for them is important for successful leadership.

The economic downturn of the early 2000s, sometimes called the "Great Recession," brought an unprecedented level of financial chaos to public higher education in America. Programs were reduced, furloughs and layoffs were common, class sizes were increased, class offerings and sections were cut, and many students couldn't get into the classes they needed for graduation (Jones & Wellman, 2010). Policy makers were more willing to allow tuition costs for students and families to increase than they were to raise taxes to meet the shortfall.

As Jones and Wellman point out (2010), higher education has been through difficult economic times before the Great Recession. The pattern of the past two decades has been a zigzag of reductions in state funds for higher education during times of recession, followed by a return to revenue growth about two years after recovery. But resources have never returned to pre-recession levels. The result is an unsteady but continual state disinvestment in higher education.

Per-student spending on higher education fell to less than $5,900 in the fiscal year 2012, a 9.1 percent decrease from 2011 and a quarter-century low for the third consecutive year (Kelderman, 2013). As state support of higher education went down, the share of revenue coming from student tuition increased substantially. And the proportion of spending for instructional function of higher education went down as institutions resorted to a greater use of part-time faculty to insulate themselves from the negative effects of budget instability. The net consequences of state disinvestment in higher education have been growth in tuition dependency, reductions in access that fall most heavily on low-income and first-generation students, and budget cuts that fall most heavily on the instructional function of the colleges and universities (Jones & Wellman, 2010). Community colleges, however, concentrated what money they had on instruction (Mullin, 2010). They spent 44.5 percent of education and general funds on instruction compared to 39.6 percent at private research institutions and 36.1 percent at public research institutions.

The Great Recession of the early 2000s was one of the major factors contributing to a national spotlight on community colleges (Boggs, 2011). Factory closures and layoffs sent large numbers of displaced workers back to community colleges, where they hoped to pick up the skills they needed to be reemployed. Major network television news stories and newspapers highlighted community colleges that were offering discounted tuition, midnight classes, and onsite counseling to the unemployed. By fall 2010, community college leaders also were reporting a significant increase in enrollments of younger students whose parents may have sent these recent high school graduates off to a university in better economic times. In fact, the American Institutes for Research found that, during the recession, the number of first-time, full-time, degree- or certificate-seeking community college students increased (Schneider & Yin, 2011).

Between 2008 and 2010, credit enrollment in community colleges surged by 17 percent (Mullin & Phillippe, 2009). At the same time that community college student enrollment was surging, most states were responding to the economic downturn by cutting funding support. Although federal stimulus funding, provided by the American Recovery and Reinvestment Act (ARRA) of 2009, provided temporary assistance to the states, the effects of the severe economic recession of the first decade of the 2000s lingered, creating significant problems for college leaders who were trying to respond to increased enrollment pressure with significantly less funding. The Center for American Progress documented that the amount of funding public colleges received from state governments as a share of total revenue declined sharply during the recession (Bergeron, Baylor, & Flores, 2014). Between fiscal years 2003 and 2010, state funding declined from 30.9 to 22.3 percent of total revenue, with the cuts disproportionately affecting community colleges. By 2011, however, some state policy makers began to protect community colleges from some of the most severe cuts (Moltz, 2011).

During the Great Recession, eleven states decreased higher education funding by more than 30 percent, and seventeen states saw decreases between 20 and 30 percent. After an initial enrollment surge, colleges could not accommodate the additional student demand, and enrollment began to decline. Reports of students being turned away or not being able to enroll in the classes they needed made national news in 2009 and 2010. California lost more than half a million community college students in the Great Recession because of state funding cuts (Katsinas et al., 2014).

Reductions in state funding coincided with increased reliance on student tuition revenue (Bergeron et al., 2014). For public colleges and universities, reductions in state support have been the primary impetus for tuition cost increases for students. However, increased tuition revenue usually does not completely make up for the loss of state revenue. Alabama's community colleges saw state funding cuts of more than 40 percent during the recession, while tuition increased just 9 percent (Katsinas et al., 2014). One method that public colleges and universities began to utilize increasingly to offset revenue loss was to escalate recruitment of higher-paying international and out-of-state students. By 2014, out-of-state students at the University of California had reached 20.2 percent of entering freshmen ("More Out-of-State Students," 2014). Although higher education leaders made the case that the revenue from out-of-state students helped them to meet operational costs, the rapid increase in numbers of out-of-state students generated a backlash. Kiley (2013) reported that the focus on out-of-state enrollments has resulted in a decreased proportion of in-state, low-income, and underrepresented minority students who are accepted at universities. Policy makers have questioned higher education leaders about the appearance that out-of-state and international students are displacing the very students that the institutions were built to serve.

Funding problems, of course, didn't start with the economic downturn of the first decade of the 2000s. The trend toward state disinvestment in higher education has been ongoing even in good economic times (Policy Research Institute, 2010), and community colleges have been the higher education institutions most affected because of their reliance on taxpayer support. In a 2010 report from the American Association of Community Colleges (AACC), *Doing More With Less: The Inequitable Funding of Community Colleges*, Christopher Mullin (2010) pointed out that, although community colleges serve 43 percent of all undergraduates (54 percent of all undergraduates in public higher education), they receive only 27 percent of total federal, state, and local higher education revenues. Community colleges are asked to educate the students who are most at risk with the least support, by far, of any other sector. If the United States is to meet the challenges of the future, policy makers must provide needed and more equitable support to colleges and universities and their students. Education, at all levels, must be seen as an important state and federal investment in our future, and policies must be put in place to ensure maximum return on that investment. Community college leaders must be prepared to become even more assertive in their advocacy for necessary public support.

Saving for Retirement

Changes in accounting rules can sometimes present significant issues for college leaders. For example, the Government Accountability Standards Board (GASB) now requires employers who provide defined benefit pensions to recognize a pension liability and deferred outflows of resources to be recorded on annual audits (GASB 68). College leaders who believed they had comfortable financial reserves were sometimes surprised to see these funds disappear into a restricted account to fund retiree compensation. Similarly, colleges that provide health benefits for retirees now have to establish accounts to fund them. In California, the Community College League of California has established a Joint Powers Agreement to assist the colleges to fund this liability.

Even in states that have statewide pension systems, the poor return on investments during the economic downturn has caused concerns about the viability of the systems to fund future retirees. The likely outcome will be increased contributions into the systems on the part of both employees and the colleges.

Tuition Increases and College Costs

Although tuition increases in the for-profit sector may be a result of increases in federal financial aid and the effect of the regulation that no more than 90 percent of revenues can come from Title IV federal student aid sources, state disinvestment in higher education has been the primary driver of tuition increases in public institutions. Because of a widespread concern that the rising costs of higher education are making college unaffordable for many students and their families, the US Government Accountability Office (GAO) was asked to study state policies affecting affordability. Federal and state support is central to promoting college affordability; however, persistent state budget constraints have limited funding for public colleges (GAO, 2014).

In 1987, net tuition revenue paid for 23 percent of the educational costs at public institutions of higher education. In 2001, tuition was a little more than a third of the costs (Kelderman, 2013). From fiscal years 2003 through 2012, state funding for all public colleges decreased, while tuition costs rose. Specifically, state funding decreased by 12 percent overall while median tuition costs rose 55 percent across all public colleges. Tuition revenue for public colleges increased from 17 percent to 25 percent, surpassing state funding by fiscal year 2012. Correspondingly, average net tuition, which is the estimated tuition after grant aid is deducted, also increased by 19 percent during this period. These increases have contributed to the decline in college affordability as students and their families are bearing the cost of college as a larger portion of their total family budgets (GAO, 2014).

According to the public policy organization Demos, average tuition at four-year public universities increased nationally by 20 percent in the four years between 2008 and 2012 after rising 14 percent in the four years prior. In seven states, average tuition increased by more than a third during this eight-year period, and two states—Arizona and California— have raised it by more than 66 percent. At public community colleges, average tuition rose by more than a third in six states during that period. Average tuition at four-year public schools by 2014 consumed more than 15 percent of the median household income in 26 states. Average total cost of a college education—including room and board—consumed more than one-third of the median household income in 23 states.

The Demos report claimed that the decreasing affordability of higher education has eroded the last relatively secure path into the middle class in America as more students took on larger amounts of debt to finance their higher educations—or gave up on college altogether. With $1.2 trillion in student loan debt outstanding and climbing, student loan debt was, by 2014, substantial enough to affect the overall economy as indebted graduates found it harder to purchase a home or a car (Hiltonsmith & Draut, 2014).

Beth Akers and Matthew Chingos (2014), however, made a case that the burden of student indebtedness has not increased significantly. After analyzing more than two decades of data on the financial well-being of American households, they argued that the impact of student loans may not be as dire as many commentators fear. The authors of this Brookings Institution report drew on data from the Survey of Consumer Finances (SCF) administered by the Federal Reserve Board to track how the education debt levels and incomes of young households evolved between 1989 and 2010. Their analysis produced three particularly noteworthy findings:

1. Roughly one quarter of the increase in student debt between 1989 and 2010 can be directly attributed to the fact that Americans were obtaining more education, especially graduate degrees. The average debt levels of borrowers with graduate degrees more than quadrupled, from just under $10,000 to more than $40,000. By

comparison, the debt loads of those with only a bachelor's degree increased by a smaller margin, from $6,000 to $16,000.

2. Increases in the average lifetime incomes of college-educated Americans have more than kept pace with increases in debt loads. Between 1992 and 2010, the average household with student debt saw an increase of about $7,400 in annual income and $18,000 in total debt. The increase in earnings received over the course of 2.4 years would pay for the increase in debt incurred.

3. The monthly payment burden faced by student loan borrowers has stayed about the same or even lessened over the two decades of the study. The median borrower consistently spent 3 to 4 percent of monthly income on student loan payments since 1992, and the mean payment-to-income ratio fell significantly, from 15 to 7 percent. The average repayment term for student loans increased over this period, allowing borrowers to shoulder increased debt loads without larger monthly payments.

Affordability

Community college leaders are typically concerned about the costs to attend college and are reluctant to recommend increases in tuition costs for students. The colleges enroll the most economically challenged students in all of higher education, and they often have difficulty meeting the costs of textbooks, tuition, transportation, and living expenses. According to a 2015 survey of more than four thousand students at ten community colleges across the nation, half of all community college students struggle with food and/or housing insecurity. Fully 20 percent are hungry, and 13 percent are homeless (Goldrick-Rab, Broton, & Eisenberg, 2015).

America's Promise

In early 2014, President Barack Obama proposed a federal incentive for states to provide free tuition for students who attend community colleges at least half time and who remain in good academic standing. The proposal is modeled after a program that was initiated in Tennessee. Although community college leaders generally reacted enthusiastically to the president's proposal, it has not been embraced by other sectors of higher education. In particular, for-profit colleges, which have already been the subject of criticism by the Obama administration for costs and low completion rates, may see this support of public community colleges as providing them an unfair competitive advantage. Publicly funded state colleges and universities may view the president's proposal as a threat to their lower-division enrollment.

Of course, President Obama's proposal for free community college tuition has a long way to go even if it is enacted, and some congressional Republicans have criticized it as unwarranted federal intrusion into an issue that should be the prerogative of the states. Also, it should be noted that community college tuition costs are already much lower than they are in any other segment of American higher education, and tuition charges constitute only a portion of what it costs to go to college.

Responses to Economic Cycles

Jones and Wellman (2010) observed that both state governments and higher education institutions have managed economic recessions largely by "muddling through," employing a combination of tuition cost increases and budget cuts to bring revenues and expenditures into balance. Enrollments are usually cut, sometimes dramatically and primarily in the community colleges, although growing demand for higher education has caused aggregate enrollments to rebound, usually within a year or two after economic recovery. But those students denied access during tough economic times don't simply postpone college entrance; most forego it and, therefore, don't acquire the skills that would benefit them or society in an increasingly competitive twenty-first-century economy.

Economic downturns are disruptive, but there are warning signs that should serve to alert leaders in time to plan for them. Although the American Recovery and Reinvestment Act of 2009 provided temporary stability to many higher education institutions, policy analysts were concerned about the "fiscal cliff" that would result when the federal funds were lost before the economy had recovered. Leaders who had developed multiyear budget scenarios were able to take action, where legally allowed, to build financial reserves, delay expenditures, freeze replacement of noncritical positions, hold the line on granting employee salary and benefit increases, and offer early retirement incentives to the highest salaried employees in order to decrease costs. The colleges that suffered less disruption during the economic downturn had leaders who anticipated it and made decisions that, although difficult and perhaps unpopular, benefitted the institutions, their students, and their employees.

A difficult economy often provides opportunities for changes that might be more difficult in better economic times. Difficult financial periods can be the best time to focus on an institution's core mission, to discontinue programs that are least aligned to the mission, to eliminate waste and duplication, to improve efficiency, and to build a stronger private fundraising function. In a personal interview with George Boggs in 2011, Jack Scott, then chancellor of the California community colleges, said that the lack of resources required colleges to prioritize. He believed that colleges needed to put transfer courses, career and technical programs, and basic skills programs as the first priorities. In tough times, he believed that personal enrichment courses had to be eliminated as not being part of the core mission. However, where colleges have to rely on the passage of operational tax levies, cutting personal enrichment programs may carry political risk.

As the economy recovers and funds are restored, college leaders have an opportunity to allocate the new resources to new programs and services. Instead of rebuilding or restoring programs that were reduced or eliminated during the downturn, colleges can strengthen or build programs and services that better meet the needs of students and communities, better match the needs of local employers, or have the potential for increasing student success rates and closing achievement gaps.

College leaders need to be careful not to create any unfunded future liabilities or to commit one-time funds to ongoing expenses. Planning to meet expenses that might be imposed by the state, such as increased contributions to pension systems, and to meet expenses for deferred maintenance is critical to a leader's success. College CEOs need to have competent fiscal and facilities administrators in their administrations.

Fundraising and Entrepreneurialism

A case can be made for the need for public institutions of higher education not only to improve advocacy efforts but also to become less reliant on public funding and to develop new revenue streams. In 2014, public higher education fell as a funding priority for states across the country (Katsinas et al., 2014). Issues that are competing with higher education for funding at the state level are unfunded state pensions, Medicaid and other health care costs related to the federal Affordable Care Act, tax reductions, transportation and highway maintenance, and corrections. There is no evidence that these competing priorities will diminish in the future.

As pointed out by the American Association of Community Colleges, advocacy is an important competency for community college leaders. Leaders will need to make the strongest case possible for support of their institutions and their students. To help college leaders to deliver a compelling message focused on the importance of greater support, the American

Association of Community Colleges has created customizable print adver-
tisements, an op-ed template, a fact sheet, advocacy radio scripts, and a
social media guide that help member colleges make their case before state
legislatures and key audiences. The pieces are customizable to fit local
college needs and focus on key community college issues (AACC, 2011).

In an environment of declining public resources and demands to do
more with less, it is essential that community colleges become even more
entrepreneurial. Their programs and services must be high quality, but
that is not enough to excel—the best community colleges will be the most
flexible and adaptive. Some colleges have focused more attention on
revenue-generating programs and services, such as providing contract
training to business and industry or to government or the military. Some
have built corporate colleges or designed facilities to provide these types
of revenue-generating programs and services. Others have built university centers, leasing facilities for four-year institutions to offer classes
more conveniently. Colleges with unused land or facilities may be able to
enter into long-term lease arrangements with businesses, government
agencies, or other educational institutions to generate revenue. Partnerships with these organizations may yield joint-use facilities such as
libraries or athletic playing fields that benefit the college.

As Roueche and Jones (2005) point out, the idea of the entrepreneurial
college is not merely about making money but making things happen and
developing resources so the college can meet the needs of students and
communities. Some of the examples of entrepreneurialism that the authors
highlight do not generate any funds, but they expand the capabilities of the
institution. Public–private partnerships are emerging as a popular form of
entrepreneurialism. Several colleges have hired consulting firms to assist
with planning, accreditation responses, reorganization, trustee development,
and other issues in which an objective view can provide the impetus for the
college to improve and make necessary changes. Colleges are increasingly
contracting with private firms to operate auxiliary services such as book-
stores and food services, allowing college personnel to focus their efforts
on the education and support services that are most important to their
students. Of course, it is important that a college's entrepreneurial activities
are compatible with and contribute to its mission and values.

Fundraising—a long-established activity at four-year institutions—is
becoming a necessity, rather than an option, for community colleges
struggling to maintain their missions. Colleges are also turning to foundations and partnering more with business and industry for financial
and in-kind support and opportunities to enhance student success and
graduation rates. Even though community colleges have been late to the

fundraising business, the potential is there to be successful. If a college does not have a foundation, the first step is to establish one. Employing a full-time foundation director who is an experienced fundraiser and providing a budget for staff support is essential. Ideally, the foundation director should report to the college president in order to have the necessary status to be effective. Donors most often want to present their gifts directly to the president. Funding and staffing a grants office is important if a college is to be effective in securing grant funds to support specific programs. Many colleges have been successful in campaigns for levies for operations and for bond funds to build or repair facilities. Each of these efforts requires the time and commitment of the president and the support of the college and community leadership.

Strong and creative leadership is, of course, important, but the entrepreneurial and fundraising culture must pervade the institution. Often the college leaders are not so much creators as they are collaborators, supporters, facilitators, consensus makers, and incentive providers—and they must continually acknowledge the accomplishments and contributions of others while encouraging risk-taking (Roueche & Jones, 2005).

Performance-Based Funding

Public higher education has traditionally been funded by states using a workload measure based upon student enrollment, usually calculated in terms of full-time student equivalent enrollment, to account for part-time students. The principle behind an enrollment-driven funding formula is that institutional costs for instruction, services, and facilities depend upon enrollment. States usually developed a system to provide a base level of funding to small colleges because of economies of scale that were possible at larger institutions. From an accountability perspective, institutions are rewarded under the traditional funding system by increasing enrollment, although some states constrained the rate of growth through the use of enrollment caps. Access to higher education, especially for community colleges, is a significant institutional value. Colleges generally focus marketing efforts on getting the right number of students into classes before they are counted during a specified census period for state apportionment. There is generally no direct financial incentive to institutions for retaining students beyond the census period.

With the increased concern for college completion, state policy makers have begun to shift funding formulas to reward state policy goals. Funding based upon outcomes established by policy makers is called performance-based funding. Performance-based funding was first tried by the Tennessee Higher Education Commission in 1978. After a slow start, the outcomes-based model for funding spread to twenty-six states by 2000 (Harnish, 2011). Many of these early funding formulas applied only to "new money" rather than base funding. When the economy began to decline and state budgets were cut, performance-based funding was often among the first programs to be eliminated. Even when some level of performance funding was preserved, its small percentage of the total institutional funding did not seem to improve the outcomes that were established as goals. Newer versions of performance-based funding are more focused on outcomes deemed important by the state, and they account for a greater percentage of institutional base funding.

Arguments in favor of performance-based funding are primarily based upon goals to improve a state's educational levels and the public's desire to get what it pays for. Schneider and Yin (2011) reported that state and local governments appropriated close to $3 billion to community colleges to help pay for the education of full-time, degree-seeking students who did not return for a second year. When financial aid is added, almost $4 billion in federal, state, and local taxpayer monies in appropriations and student grants went to first-year community college dropouts. Proponents of performance-based funding believe that the public should not be paying this much for failure.

Some of those who argue against performance-based funding believe it is another effort on the part of state policy makers to cut funding. Others are concerned that financially rewarding completion instead of access will penalize institutions in high-poverty areas with the students who are most at risk, while rewarding institutions that serve a student population that is more likely to succeed. Still others believe it will shift the mission of the institutions to the point that underprepared students will lose access or that quality will suffer in an effort to move students through to completion.

Nonetheless, performance-based funding has been spreading as the economy has improved and as state policy makers become more concerned about accountability for college completion. The Education Policy Center at the University of Alabama reported that twenty-two states have performance-based funding systems in place, seven are currently transitioning to performance-based funding, and ten additional states have had formal discussions about performance-based funding (Friedel et al., 2013). The Policy Center's report describes the models that have been developed in several states. Educators should help to shape the models so that potential negative consequences are minimized.

Issues to Consider

A. What steps should leaders take to prepare for an economic downturn? Which governance processes should be engaged in developing a financial plan?

B. What can be done during an economic downturn to strengthen an institution and position it to take the best advantage of an economic recovery?

C. How should leaders decide which programs and services to restore and which new programs and services to offer when the economy recovers? What criteria should be used? What governance processes should be used?

D. What are the advantages and disadvantages of employing a greater percentage of adjunct faculty members? Can college leaders address the disadvantages effectively? Is there a limit to the percentage of adjunct faculty members that an institution should employ?

E. Does the additional funding from out-of-state and international students enable higher education institutions to enroll more in-state students, or are in-state students displaced by increased numbers of out-of-state and international students?

F. How can college leaders best advocate for funding priority for their institution? What arguments can leaders make? Who should be involved in advocacy efforts?

G. What can be done to assist the students who are insecure about housing or food?

Case Scenario

The governor and legislature have reached a budget agreement that completely eliminates state funding for your college district, leaving only local property tax support and student tuition as sources of funding. You and your governing board members would like to keep both tuition costs and taxes as low as possible. But you also need to protect the quality of educational and support services for your students. What issues does the scenario create? What leadership competencies are involved? Who should be involved in addressing the situation? What actions would you take? Are there lessons to be learned?

H. What are the advantages of a system of free tuition for community college students? If students don't have to pay to attend, will they have the necessary motivation to persist in their studies?

I. What is an example of an entrepreneurial activity at a community college? How much risk is associated with entrepreneurial activity, and how can it be minimized?

REFERENCES

Akers, B., & Chingos, M. (2014). *Is a Student Loan Crisis on the Horizon?* Washington, DC: Brookings Institution. June 24, 2014. Retrieved from http://www.brookings.edu/research/reports/2014/06/24-student-loan-crisis-akers-chingos.

American Association of Community Colleges. (2011). *Advocacy Toolkit.* Washington, DC: Author. Retrieved from http://www.aacc.nche.edu/Advocacy/toolkit/Pages/default.aspx.

Baum, S., Ma, J., & Payea, K. (2013). *Education Pays 2013: The Benefits of Higher Education for Individuals and Society.* Trends in Higher Education Series. Washington, DC: College Board. Retrieved from http://trends.collegeboard.org/sites/default/files/education-pays-2013-full-report-022714.pdf.

Bergeron, D., Baylor, E., & Flores, A. (2014). *A Great Recession, A Great Retreat: A Call for a Public College Quality Compact.* Washington, DC: Center for American Progress. October. Retrieved from http://cdn.americanprogress.org/wp-content/uploads/2014/10/PublicCollege-report.pdf.

Boggs, G. (2011). Community Colleges in the Spotlight and under the Microscope. *New Directions for Community Colleges* (No.156), 3–22.

Economic Modeling Specialists, International. (2007). *Engines of Prosperity: America's Community and Technical Colleges.* Moscow, ID: Author.

Friedel, J., Thornton, Z., D'Amico, M., & Katsinas, S. (2103). *Performance-Based Funding: The National Landscape.* Tuscaloosa, AL: University of Alabama Education Policy Center. Retrieved from http://uaedpolicy.ua.edu/uploads/2/1/3/2/21326282/pbf_9–17_web.pdf.

Government Accountability Office. (2014). *Higher Education State Funding Trends and Policies on Affordability.* Washington, DC: Author. GAO-15–151. Retrieved from http://www.gao.gov/assets/670/667557.pdf.

Goldrick-Rab, S., Broton, K., & Eisenberg, D. (2015). *Hungry to Learn: Addressing Food and Housing Insecurity Among Undergraduates.* Madison, WI: Wisconsin Hope Lab. Retrievable from http://wihopelab .com/publications/Wisconsin_hope_lab_hungry_to_learn.pdf.

Harnish, T. (2011). *Performance-Based Funding: A Re-emerging Strategy in Public Higher Education Financing.* Washington, DC: American Association of State Colleges and Universities.

Hiltonsmith, R., & Draut, T. (2014). *The Great Cost Shift Continues: State Education Funding After the Recession.* New York, NY: Demos. Retrieved from http://www.demos.org/sites/default/files/publications/TheGreat CostShift2014-Brief_0.pdf.

Jones, D., & Wellman, J. (2010). Breaking Bad Habits: Navigating the Financial Crisis. *Change, 42*(3), 6–13. Retrieved from http://www.changemag.org/ Archives/Back%20Issues/May-June%202010/breaking-bad-full.html.

Katsinas, S. G., Shedd, L. E., Adair, J. L., Malley, M. S., Koh, J. P., & Lacey, V. A., D'Amico, M. M., & Friedel, J. N. (2014). *Recovery Continues, but Competition Is Fierce.* Tuscaloosa, AL: University of Alabama Education Policy Center.

Kelderman, E. (2013, March 6). Students and States Near a 50–50 Split on the Cost of Public Higher Education. *Chronicle of Higher Education.* Retrieved from http://chronicle.com/article/StudentsStates-Near-a/137709/.

Kiley, K. (2013, April 30). Crowded Out. *Inside Higher Ed.* Retrieved from https://www.insidehighered.com/news/2013/04/30/out-state-enrollment- decreases-minority-low-income-student-enrollment.

Moltz, D. (2011, March 31). Triage Funding for Community Colleges. *Inside Higher Ed.* Retrieved from http://www.insidehighered.com/ news/2011/03/31/state_budgets_and_community_college_funding.

More Out-of-State Students at U. of California. (2014, July 23). *Inside Higher Ed.* Retrieved from https://www.insidehighered.com/quicktakes/ 2014/07/23/more-out-state-students-u-california.

Mullin, C. (2010) *Doing More With Less: The Inequitable Funding of Community Colleges.* AACC Policy Brief 2010–03PBL. Washington, DC: American Association of Community Colleges. Retrieved from http://www. aacc.nche.edu/Publications/Briefs/Pages/rb09082010.aspx.

Mullin, C. (2011). *A Sound Investment: The Community College Dividend.* Washington, DC: American Association of Community Colleges (AACC Policy Brief 2011-01PBL). Retrieved from http://www.aacc.nche.edu/ Publications/Briefs/Documents/2011–01PBL_Investment.pdf.

80 PRACTICAL LEADERSHIP IN COMMUNITY COLLEGES

Mullin, C., & Phillippe, K. (2009). *Community College Enrollment Surge: An Analysis of Estimated Fall 2009 Headcount Enrollments at Community Colleges*. Policy Brief 2009–01 PBL. Washington, DC: American Association of Community Colleges. Retrieved from http://www.aacc.nche.edu/Publications/Briefs/Pages/rb12172009.aspx.

Policy Research Institute. (2010). *How to Fix a Broken System: Funding Public Higher Education and Making It More Productive: Setting a Pathway to Greater Productivity Within New Funding Realities*. Princeton: New Jersey Association of State Colleges and Universities. Retrieved from http://www.njascu.org/PolicyBriefApril2010.pdf.

Roueche, J., & Jones, B. (2005). *The Entrepreneurial College*. Washington, DC: Community College Press.

Schneider, M., & Yin, L. (2011). *The Hidden Costs of Community Colleges*. Washington, DC: American Institutes of Research. Retrieved from http://www.air.org/sites/default/files/downloads/report/AIR_Hidden_Costs_of_Community_Colleges_Oct2011_0.pdf.

5

DIVERSITY, EQUITY,
AND INCLUSION

Beyond the Open Door

Effective management of diversity, equity, and inclusion (DEI) is a major key to the future sustainability of the American community college. No longer can community college educators hide behind the historic open-door admission policies, suggesting that open access policies alone are sufficient to provide for the educational needs of all students. Today's community college leaders must embrace diversity, equity, and inclusion in all aspects of their leadership. Community colleges can no longer be about only access and opportunity; today's college leaders must examine how their students are treated and what support structures are in place to accommodate their needs in order to improve success rates and close achievement gaps. In the twenty-first-century community college, management of issues involving diversity, equity, and inclusion is an urgent educational imperative.

Some community college leaders pay lip service to diversity, equity, and inclusion, and they may not necessarily have institutionalized the policies and procedures to make these values real. DEI is more than measuring student and employee demographics and support for a few special programs and services. America and the local communities served by community colleges are changing, and the new populations of students and employees carefully evaluate how the institution relates to them. If community colleges do not connect with them in a relevant manner, they will begin to question the institution's authenticity and relevancy. John Brooks Slaughter, the first African American director of the National Science Foundation and a distinguished academic leader is quoted as saying:

> It must be recognized that American higher education is a microcosm of American society. It possesses all the strengths and possibilities as

well as all the weaknesses and pathologies of our nation. Just as America continues to be a "work in progress," higher education is evolving as well. It is this evolution that must be guided and nurtured by those who understand the essential role that our colleges and universities play in improving our society. (Slaughter, 2004)

Understanding DEI

The persistence of educational disparities in the community college sector makes the concepts of diversity, equity, and inclusion important. If leaders are to be successful, DEI values must be embedded in the culture of the college. The mission of the college must clearly state that diversity, equity, and inclusion are essential institutional values. Commitments to DEI focus educators on the needs of all of the people connected to the college in a holistic way. Diversity, equity, and inclusion can be thought of as "linked" concepts that drive the work of the community college.

1. Diversity is usually measured by the elements that categorize groups and people (Grodsky & Kurlaender, 2010). Today, most community colleges have ways to track ethnicity, gender, and age of their students. In reality, diversity is much more than quantifying these differences. The advantages of institutional diversity are unlocked when institutions establish and sustain policies and practices that respect, appreciate, protect, and value differences while creating opportunities for students and employees to learn from one another.

2. Equity in higher education, according to Bensimon and Polkinghorne (2003), means equal access to and success in higher education among historically underrepresented student populations, such as ethnic minority and low-income students. Bensimon defines three components of equity: (1) representational equity, which refers to the proportional participation of historically underrepresented student populations at all levels of an institution; (2) resource equity, which takes into account the proportion of educational resources that are directed at closing equity gaps; and (3) equity mindedness, which refers to the priority that the institution gives to equity efforts. The concepts of diversity, equity, and inclusion require institutional leaders and staff to demonstrate both awareness and a willingness to address differences by instituting policies and practices to serve all students.

3. Inclusion is a value that commits an institution to provide all people at the institution with opportunities for academic and personal success. In particular, inclusion is about making sure that all students feel welcome and that their unique needs and learning styles are attended to and valued by the institution (Dougherty & Kienzl, 2006). Inclusive community colleges are democratic institutions that clearly demonstrate why the American community college was established. Inclusion is at the core of the development of the community college movement and how the college should conduct all of its business.

The successful twenty-first-century community college leader needs to attend to all three of these concepts of diversity, equity, and inclusion to ensure that their institutions are relevant and that all students learn the values of our multicultural democracy. More and more community college leaders are adding diversity, equity, and inclusion to their strategic plans, and it's long overdue. Outdated policies and practices prevent colleges from realizing the full potential of a diverse and inclusive institution. Many organizations may still be focused only on counting the numbers. Although diversity in higher education is increasingly respected as a fundamental characteristic (Cohen & Brawer, 1996), many community colleges have yet to link diversity with equity and inclusion. The combination of the three concepts enhances the college's ability to achieve meaningful outcomes for underrepresented students and employees. Colleges can demonstrate equity and inclusion by engaging people from diverse backgrounds, treating them fairly, and including their perspectives in the way the college conducts its business.

Institutionalizing DEI

The community colleges leaders who are bold enough to embrace diversity, equity, and inclusion as institutional core values will reap enormous benefits in an improved institutional climate and in the success of students. The first step is to transition from the single concept of diversity (provided by the open-door policy) to the combined concepts of equity and inclusion (provided by behavior and practices). In other words, the institutions must shift from focusing only on student and employee demographics to transforming attitudes, behaviors, policies, and practices. When diversity and equity are practiced at the college, stakeholders' behavior demonstrates engagement and support for the mission. A diverse and inclusive environment enables all stakeholders to contribute their full potential in pursuit of the college's goals. The DEI environment involves the celebration of various cultures, religions, and ethnicities. Colleges can sponsor cultural educational opportunities that provide students, faculty, and staff with skills and knowledge to become competent global citizens. It is imperative that community colleges employ policies and practices that embrace and support diversity, equity, and inclusion (American Association of Community Colleges [AACC], 2014).

Why DEI Efforts Fail

Launching a DEI agenda may inspire both positive and negative responses at a college. Efforts to reach underserved populations require institutions to alter their policies and practices. In most cases, DEI efforts also require the institutions to push for behavioral changes from their employees. Helping entrenched faculty and staff to change is difficult. For some community college leaders, implementing programs in diversity, equity, and inclusion may bring about added concerns to an already full plate of competing programs and leadership challenges.

Some entrenched community college educators may dismiss newly launched DEI efforts because they have witnessed the development of numerous other leadership initiatives that did not go anywhere. They might see the diversity, equity, and inclusion efforts as just another passing fad. Further, in some cases, faculty and administrators may view equity efforts as a path to lower academic standards in order to accommodate disadvantaged students. One of the first concerns that some leaders express when considering the prospect of adding DEI to the college's agenda is fitting additional programs into an already underfunded environment. Unfortunately, many well-meaning DEI initiatives fail because organizations push them only as a compliance issue. In other situations, the DEI effort is an appendage program that is never mentioned in the college's strategic plan. Some institutions develop college-wide programs to increase diversity without necessary stakeholder input and buy-in.

Few leaders see diversity, equity, and inclusion as a compendium that creates a democratic institution but instead measure or target them individually. Despite the many benefits of diversity, as colleges embrace DEI they often realize that the idea of launching the efforts comes with many unintended issues and concerns. Sometimes when the workplace becomes increasingly diverse, employees' dissimilarity increases, and entrenched faculty and staff may feel uncomfortable dealing with diverse populations (Moody, 2004).

DEI Issues

There are several common DEI issues that leaders must acknowledge and manage. Perhaps most critical are issues involving classroom teaching practices. Community college educators and researchers are calling for change in teaching practices in order to address the needs of diverse learners (Barr & Tagg, 1995; Border & Chism, 1992; Goodwin & Miller, 2013). These authors advocate changes in the alignment of classroom and institutional practices to better serve students. They argue that the institution must be sensitive to the different learning styles of the students. Before teaching academic material, the instructor's primary responsibility is to meet four basic needs of all students: (1) the need to feel welcome, (2) the need to be treated as individuals, (3) the need to feel they can participate fully, and (4) the need to be treated fairly.

Davis (2009) warns teachers not to try to match their teaching styles to all their students' learning styles, but rather to help students become more aware of their learning strategies. Davis recommends that when designing or revising a course, faculty must consider what material to teach, how best to teach it, and how to ensure that students are learning what is being taught. Davis cautions that "many instructors, hoping to impart to students everything they know about a subject, attempt to include far too much material. Indeed, one of the most difficult steps in planning a course is deciding which topics must be excluded if the whole is to be manageable" (pp.75–76).

Her advice on teaching students with disabilities, reentry students, academically diverse students, and other disadvantaged students can be used to help improve the teaching and learning environment for a diverse group of learners. Goebel (1995) examined differences in learning and communication styles that relate to gender, class, and ethnicity. For example, cultural groups that value individualism may perform well in classrooms where students enter heated debates with each other and the instructor. Students may resist the teacher's goals when learning styles are at odds. McPhail, McPhail, and Smilkstein (2001) expanded on the importance of looking at classroom practice by focusing on culturally mediated instruction. Culturally diverse students, especially African Americans, are not generally successful in classrooms that ignore cultural differences (McPhail & McPhail, 1999). The theory of culturally mediated education explains the conceptual basis of the learning and student-centered paradigms. For example, students from different cultures have different cognitive styles and different cognitive ways of processing information and knowledge. Culturally diverse students can become successful learners when cultural differences are taken into account in the classroom.

Uri Treisman, professor of mathematics and director of the Charles A. Dana Center at the University of Texas at Austin, demonstrated that African American learners could excel by establishing a learning environment of high expectations and peer support. According to Treisman (1992), African American students in his calculus classes at the University of California at Berkeley were not successful primarily because they studied independently and separated themselves from other learners. He examined student behaviors of different cultural groups to determine the effect of behaviors on student academic performance. He found that the key to student success was to build a community of learners, focused on the study of mathematics, to create a supportive merging of academic and social lives for learners. Treisman successfully replicated his student study group experiments with an honors program that focused on collaborative learning and the use of small-group teaching methods.

Campus Climate Issues

Structures, policies, and practices influence the college's campus climate (Chang, 2000). The demographics of students and employees as well as the attitudes and values of its members and leaders influence campus climate. By blending diversity, equity, and inclusion into its culture, the college can focus on the needs of every individual. College leaders and trustees should create policies and practices to ensure that the right conditions are in place for all stakeholders to achieve their full potential.

The heightened awareness and acceptance of difference through diversity and inclusion initiatives can underscore the college's commitment to making sure that all students feel welcome. Smith (2000) explains that campus climate addresses the collegiate environment on institutional, faculty, and student success and includes activities that seek to prevent faculty and students from finding their campuses alienating. Typically, the more included the stakeholders from all backgrounds feel on campus, the warmer the campus climate. Higher education researchers refer to "campus climate" to describe a particular college or university's culture and habits toward inclusion of all members and constituencies. Cabrera, Nora, Terenzini, Pascarella, and Hagedorn (1999) indicated that both minorities and nonminorities adjust to college in a similar manner. For both groups, persistence is determined by preparation for college, positive academic experiences, strong parental encouragement, and academic performance in college. For both groups, exposure to a campus climate of prejudice and intolerance lessens commitment to the institution and indirectly weakens decisions to persist. These authors suggest that broad-based policies and practices need to be implemented to overcome stereotypes. College administrators can diffuse racial tension by creating a climate that fosters tolerance. Strategies to enhance tolerance include cultural awareness workshops, multicultural education, collaborative learning classroom practices, faculty training on cultural diversity, and culturally sensitive hiring practices.

Chang (2000) noted that although virtually all colleges and universities recognize the need to improve racial dynamics, colleges often fail to examine how their racial endeavors are affected by or affect other institutional policies and practices. Problems may be caused by not paying enough attention to factors such as values, ideals, expectations, or practices and by competition with opposing institutional interests. The conflicts that often arise have very real consequences that can potentially obstruct racial progress by neutralizing even the most promising efforts toward diversity. Pettigrew (1994) describes and defines prejudice and discrimination as being direct or indirect and intentional or unintentional. He describes how campus policies can reduce prejudice. Pettigrew states that the focus on changing intergroup norms is more useful than general concern about campus climate and that intergroup climates emerge from the normative structures established by an institution's leaders.

Recruitment and Support Issues

The most successful community colleges are finding ways to incorporate employee diversity into their workplaces without disrupting college operations. Diversity, of course, means more than just race or ethnicity. Community colleges are generally diverse workplaces; employees have many different characteristics, such as religious and political beliefs, gender, ethnicity, disability, educational level, socioeconomic background, sexual orientation, and home community.

Strategies to incorporate diversity practices in a workplace start with recruiting from diverse talent pools that open the college to candidates from a variety of backgrounds. Workplace diversity is enhanced when colleges hire a sufficient number of employees from various backgrounds and experiences. College leaders often acknowledge workplace diversity as an investment toward building a better, more culturally rich environment. Although workplace diversity provides many benefits, it also poses some challenges for both leaders and employees. To reap the benefits of workplace diversity, everyone at the college must understand the challenges and know how to deal effectively with them.

One of the major issues confronting hiring or search committees for academic appointments is finding ways to expand the pool of qualified candidates to increase the potential for minority hires. After employment, institutional practices and culture may present difficulties for minorities. Aguirre (2000) pointed out that colleges and universities have been recruiting women and minorities without understanding how these individuals fit in an institution dominated by White males. Thus, recruitment has often taken place without a complete understanding of the dominant social forces in these colleges and how institutional practices may promote an environment that appears "chilly" or "alienating" for women and minorities. Trower and Chait (2002) note that bias and "chilly environment" encountered in academia are among the biggest obstacles to retaining faculty of color.

Moody (2004) pointed out that, in order to retain and promote a more diverse workforce, institutions need to welcome faculty newcomers differently. Smith (2000) argued that institutions need to progress beyond the hiring myths and adopt new hiring practices if they want to add significant numbers of minority group members to the faculty. College leaders who set out to recruit a diverse workforce, rather than settling for a homogeneous environment, open their institutions to a larger pool of qualified applicants. As a result, they increase their access to candidates who are best able to meet the needs of the institution.

Communication Issues

Communication barriers can lead to problems when leaders attempt to create a diverse workplace. For example, when a college employs a person from a different culture whose first language is not English, the new employee may experience difficulties communicating with other faculty members, administrators, and college staff. Language problems can lead to misunderstandings and a decrease in the individual's acclimation to the job. Cultural differences also can present challenges to communication. As an example, George Boggs, as a college president, had a practice of treating new faculty members individually to breakfast or lunch in their first year. The meetings were intended to see how everything was going for the new faculty member and to reinforce college values. The meeting with a faculty member who was deaf was a success—but only because the faculty member was an excellent lip reader. The meeting with a Latina faculty member was more awkward because she was unaccustomed to—and uncomfortable with—a one-on-one meeting with an unrelated male.

Leaders must be aware of the potential for cultural and communication challenges as colleges become more diverse. If a supervisor fails to provide clear instructions about a task, the employees may make mistakes when they attempt the work. Administrators can minimize these kinds of problems by hiring bilingual professionals who can mediate and reduce language and communication barriers. Leaders should also offer all employees professional development training on culture, clear communication, recruiting practices, and management to help address interpersonal issues.

Diversity among college employees can affect communication in both positive and negative ways. Language problems and cultural habits often create barriers to effective communication between groups. Workforce diversity training focused on communication can strengthen the college's relationships with student groups. For example, minority faculty members can be paired with students from their demographic groups, opening a channel for communication and making the students feel more comfortable and welcomed on the college campus.

Social integration on a college campus is not easy. The formation of cliques and exclusive social groups appears to be a natural process that can be impossible to discourage. This informal isolation generates divisions among student groups, creating a situation in which culturally diverse students avoid exposure to each other during out-of-class times. Although there is nothing fundamentally wrong with students affiliating only with others who are like themselves, it limits cultural learning and reduces the potential for sharing knowledge, skills, and experience.

Gender Bias Issues

Gender bias in the classroom can exist at the community college level (Moody, 2004) and create uncomfortable learning environments, usually for females. Classroom teachers can change their teaching behaviors and become aware of the gender bias that exists in many educational materials and texts. Faculty members, in particular, are in the best position to recognize any gender inequities and to take steps to combat bias. Far too many of the classroom examples and texts describe a world in which men are bright and powerful, but women are silent, passive, and invisible (Heilman, 2001). Heilman commented about her research on gender stereotypes, "We have shown, for example, that women, as compared to men, are less likely to be selected for male gender-typed positions, are more likely to have their performance in such positions devalued, and are given fewer opportunities for career advancement" (p. 658). Community college leaders must work to create learning environments that foster positive image information about women throughout the teaching and learning environment.

Students with Disabilities Issues

An important management responsibility in community colleges is ensuring that policies and procedures are in place to eliminate discrimination on the basis of disabilities. Community colleges are experiencing a significant enrollment growth of students with disabilities. According to Russa (2007), the number of students with disabilities accessing higher education in the future will continue to grow, with community colleges seeing the largest increases.

Reaching all students with disabilities can be challenging at times—even with community colleges' open-door admission policies—considering the costs of accommodations for students. Community colleges must identify ways to serve all students and potential students in their communities. Also, there are legal implications for institutions that fail to meet the needs of students with disabilities. Community college leaders must understand and comply with Section 504 of the federal Rehabilitation Act of 1973. This law is designed to protect the rights of individuals with disabilities in programs and activities that receive federal financial assistance from the US Department of Education (ED). If institutions fail to provide adequate accommodations, students have the right to file formal complaints through the Office of Civil Rights (OCR) and seek legal action against community colleges. Russa (2007) noted that these complaints could result in costly legal expenses and hours of personnel time.

Affirmative Action Issues

Affirmative action is an outcome of 1960s civil rights movement and is intended to provide equal opportunities for women and members of minority groups in education and employment. Affirmative action policies were seen as necessary in order to compensate for decades of racial, social, and economic disparities and to ensure institutional diversity. Higher education associations have consistently advocated for the importance of a racially diverse student body, most recently in amicus briefs submitted to the US Supreme Court on the 2003 University of Michigan cases of *Grutter v. Bollinger* and *Gratz v. Bollinger* (American Council on Education, 2002), the 2010, 2102, and 2015 cases of *Fisher v. University of Texas* (American Council on Education, 2015), and the 2013 case of

Schutte v. Coalition to Defend Affirmative Action (American Council on Education [ACE], 2013). However, referenda, court decisions, and legislative action are closing the door on the use of affirmative action policies to ensure diversity in the student body of institutions with selective admissions. The institutions are having some success in diversifying their student bodies by considering factors such as income level. But they have also become more interested in attracting a diverse group of transfer students from community colleges.

Community colleges will continue to attract the most diverse student bodies in American higher education. However, equity gaps by race persist, generating a growing interest in closing them. If we are to improve the standard of living, safety, and quality of life in our communities and maintain our nation's competitiveness, we will need everyone to be prepared to contribute. In the community college world, affirmative action is more a process than an admissions policy. Community college leaders must reach out to underrepresented populations to ensure their access to educational opportunity, to urge them to engage in campus activities, and to provide them the support they need to succeed.

Immigration Issues

By 2030, nearly one in five US workers will be an immigrant. It is imperative that immigrants have access to higher education and training opportunities, not only to increase their chances of personal success but also to ensure the economic and cultural vibrancy of local communities and the country as a whole. Community colleges are well positioned to be critical change agents in bringing out the untapped potential in our burgeoning immigrant population.

Federal immigration reform, including the DREAM Act, which would permit the children of undocumented immigrants to go to college at in-state tuition rates, has been stalled in Congress. States have widely divergent policies regarding access to higher education for this population. Some states allow students who have graduated from a high school in that state to attend college at in-state tuition rates; others require them to pay international student tuition rates or deny them access altogether. Congressional Republicans have threatened to override or retaliate against President Barack Obama's executive order allowing certain undocumented immigrants to stay in the United States legally for the remainder of his term, and court decisions have delayed its implementation.

For a large percentage of America's growing immigrant and refugee population, community colleges represent more than just another postsecondary education option. Community colleges are ideal venues to provide academic and cultural experiences, job skills training, civics education, and a range of social support services. College leaders should do what they can to assist underrepresented immigrants to have access to educational opportunities and become fully engaged in campus life in order for them to contribute fully to society.

Racial Issues

Although the majority of Black and Hispanic undergraduate students in the United States study at community colleges (AACC, 2014), Bill Moore, a professor in the Community College Leadership Program at the University of Texas at Austin (2006) declared his belief that discrimination was alive and well in the community college. Moore believed that community colleges still operated in a "good old boy" system. Moore argued that race is a difference that makes a difference.

Hailed as democracy's college (AACC, 2014), American community colleges are often regarded as the best in the world. However, community college reform initiatives implicitly suggest that the system could be much better if programs were in place to support and nurture students of color. Unfortunately, dealing with the racial crisis in America is one of the most significant challenges that both the country as a whole and community colleges face in the twenty-first century. Community colleges are a microcosm of their larger communities, and they can be a focal point to address larger societal issues. It came as no surprise to some when US Attorney General Eric Holder selected St. Louis Community College at Florissant Valley to meet with students and community leaders in an attempt to quell the most heated racial crisis in recent history—the death of Michael Brown, a Black teenager who was killed by a Ferguson police officer (Tyson, 2014).

Men of Color Issues

Because the vast majority of men of color begin their postsecondary experiences in community colleges, these institutions are critical for enhancing successful outcomes for these men. As noted by Bush and Bush (2010), community colleges are perceived by young men of color as a pathway to enhanced social and economic mobility. Students who can't afford a four-year college see the community college as their best option. But community colleges aren't necessarily serving male students of color effectively. Although community colleges serve as a primary entry into postsecondary education, access is not usually synonymous with success for men of color (Harper, 2009).

Even though community colleges have declared their dedication to serving their students and communities, recent research studies report that men of color perform lower than their White peers on every conceivable marker of success (persistence, completion, achievement, and transfer) (Harper, 2009; Harper & Harris, 2012; Harris & Wood, 2013). Results of the research suggest that efforts to facilitate student success for men of color must be intentional, strategic, guided by inquiry, and inclusive of a range of campus stakeholders (including students). Harris and Wood (2013) believe that rigorous assessment of efforts to support men of color must also occur on an ongoing basis.

In an examination of the academic performance of African American males at LaGuardia Community College in New York, Jordan (2008) found that there are many factors that influence their educational attainment. His findings reinforced the importance of personal characteristics such as self-awareness, self-consciousness, self-confidence, and commitment to shaping success. Jordan's study also revealed evidence that the college itself plays an important role in developing awareness and commitment to the success of African American males.

But the concern about the plight of the African American male in higher education extends beyond the doors of the community college all the way to the White House. In response to the situation, President Obama (White House, 2014) launched a new government partnership, My Brother's Keeper, with businesses and philanthropic support. The partnership is aimed at keeping high-risk young men of color on the right path. My Brother's Keeper is designed to address the challenges faced by minority boys and young men, who have lower graduation rates and more interaction with the criminal justice system than White boys and young men. In addition, professors and researchers at seven research centers—the Center for the Study of Race and Equity in Education (University of Pennsylvania), Minority Male Community College Collaborative (San Diego State University), Morehouse Research Institute (Morehouse College), Project MALES and the Texas Education Consortium for Male Students of Color (University of Texas at Austin), Todd Anthony Bell National Resource Center on the African-American Male (The Ohio State University), UCLA Black Male Institute (University of California, Los Angeles), and Wisconsin's Equity and Inclusion Laboratory (University of Wisconsin-Madison)—routinely study factors that affect educational, social, and occupational opportunities for boys and young men of color. The centers made four key recommendations for postsecondary institutions: (1) require all institutions to implement an institutional-level early alert system; (2) mandate that institutions conduct a self-study of student experiences and outcomes with data disaggregated by race within gender; (3) disaggregate student right-to-know data by race/ethnicity within gender; and (4) require federally designated minority-serving institutions to include the phrase, "Serving Historically Underserved Students" in their strategic plans along with stated student success goals.

In 2015, the Center for Community College Student Engagement (CCSSE) released a special study on men of color in community colleges. The report revealed major problems and challenges that community colleges face in their efforts to respond to the diverse learning needs of men of color. The CCSSE report presented data on engagement, described programs at different colleges, and posed a set of guiding questions for institutions to consider as they design and implement programs for men of color.

Veterans Issues

The majority of veterans on college campuses are nontraditional students; they are not entering straight from high school and are not dependent on their parents. Veterans are typically older than other students and have families. They will often attend multiple institutions while earning a degree, be enrolled part time, or have mixed enrollment (i.e., fluctuate between full- and part-time enrollment). Roughly 85 percent of veterans and active duty service members enrolled in undergraduate programs are twenty-four years of age or older. Nearly half of veteran students have families, either a spouse (47 percent) or children (47 percent). Despite only making up 10 to 12 percent of military personnel, women make up 27 percent of veterans enrolled in postsecondary education (Lang, Harriett, & Cadet, 2013).

But veterans still face challenges on campuses across the country. These challenges can range from a lack of camaraderie and understanding displayed by other students or faculty, difficulty obtaining credit for military training and experiences, concerns about targeted recruiting by unsuitable for-profit institutions, or burdensome state residency requirements. These obstacles can prevent veterans from returning to school or make it more difficult for them to finish their degrees. Increasingly, however, policy makers and campuses are addressing these challenges to make the transition to campus life easier for returning veterans. For example, states are offering immediate access to in-state tuition rates and supporting programs to make veterans feel part of the campus community.

Many community colleges have established Offices of Veterans Affairs, which serve veterans by offering support services and assistance as needed. The goal of these offices is to help veterans complete their education when they transition from the military to the college environment. The staff in the Veterans Affairs offices helps veterans connect with campus and community services. Resources provided by Veterans Affairs offices often include mentoring, mental health counseling, financial aid application assistance, support workshops, and a relaxing environment where veterans can study and network with other veterans.

A recent American Council on Education report, *Soldier to Student* (McBain, Kim, Cook, & Snead, 2012), revealed that higher education institutions throughout the United States have taken major steps to develop programs and services to better serve veteran and military students. ACE provides a Toolkit for Veteran Friendly Institutions. ACE suggests that though veteran friendly institutions may vary, a veteran friendly institution needs to define "veteran friendly" in a way that addresses both the institution's and the students' needs.

The Toolkit for Veteran Friendly Institutions is an online collaborative resource designed to help colleges and universities build better programs for student veterans. The toolkit highlights promising practices, including veteran-specific orientations, on-campus veteran service centers, prospective student outreach efforts, faculty training, and counseling and psychological services tailored to student veterans. It also includes video clips, profiles of student veterans programs across the United States, and a searchable database of tools and resources (https://vetfriendlytoolkit.acenet.edu/Pages/default.aspx).

Veteran friendly institutions are often listed in *Military Advanced Education (MAE)*, the leading journal of higher learning for the nation's armed forces. This publication provides information to help military personnel make informed choices about colleges and universities. Its *Guide to Military Friendly Colleges and Universities* is a list featured annually in the journal that reports measures of best practices in military and veteran education in order to provide America's men and women in uniform with the information they need to make the right choices about college (http://www.kmimediagroup.com/mae/latest).

LGBT Issues

Many sexual orientation or lesbian, gay, bisexual, and transgender (LGBT) issues are common to both community college campuses and four-year institutions. One is the "commuter campus syndrome." This syndrome, in which students attend classes but don't become involved in campus life, contributes to students' inability to establish relationships. Rankin (2003) observed that LGBT students are reluctant to "come out" because they perceive the campus climate to be hostile. Rankin pointed out that many LGBT students and employees find that they must hide significant parts of their identity from peers and others, thereby isolating themselves socially or emotionally.

The commuter campus situation also limits the chances of establishing relationships with LGBT peers or of creating a sense of LGBT community on campus (Sanlo, 1998). LGBT students living off campus with parents are especially affected, as are those working full or part time while attending college. Both situations adversely affect students' ability to become involved in campus-based LGBT activities.

A lack of institutional support services and inadequate opportunities to interact with other LGBT students, faculty, and staff may also play a significant role in these students' failure to persist. Finally, administrative barriers to the formation of LGBT student groups may interfere with these students' abilities to form contacts and friendships (Evans, Forney, & Guido-DiBrito, 1998; Sanlo, 1998). Community college leaders will need to take action to create campus environments where all students feel safe and welcome. Rankin's research revealed that some colleges are integrating LGBT issues into their ongoing strategic planning and student development initiatives, often leading to the creation of LGBT resource centers or safe space programs. She also observed that colleges are examining policies and procedures to ensure inclusive administrative polices that remove barriers that may obstruct educational opportunities for LGBT students.

Managing DEI Issues

Although workplace diversity benefits an organization as a whole, some employees and administrators may not respond positively to programs for underrepresented populations. In some cases, employees who oppose workforce diversity may reject new programs and create problems in the workplace for new diverse hires. If the college doesn't handle opposition appropriately, workplace diversity initiatives may not provide the intended benefits to the institution (Aquirre, 2000). Leaders need to explain the reasons for diversity, equity, and inclusion. Alleviating fears some people possess about workplace diversity may reduce much of the opposition (Hurtado, 2007).

The implementation process for new DEI programs may present challenges to everyone involved, and frustrations may arise because implementation is not as smooth as expected. Institutions may benefit from hiring experienced consultants who specialize in workplace diversity and inclusion to help with implementation of any new initiative. Experienced professional consultants understand the challenges and know how to handle major DEI issues.

Institutions must effectively manage the changes in policies and attitudes to make diversity work. Changing policies and practices can present a challenge for many leaders. Taking the wrong approach to solving diversity issues can create challenges for leaders. College administrators should work within the internal college governance structure to develop strategies to implement diversity plans, analyze results, and make necessary changes if results do not meet the established goals.

College leaders should consider five strategies for management and implementation of DEI issues:

1. **Build an inclusive campus environment.**

   Research shows that a diversity goal alone is not enough (Hurtado, 2007). College leaders need to work from a well-documented plan of action, complete with goals, objectives, and many small, manageable tasks to help realize change. Achieving an inclusive work environment is a culture change initiative, but it does not necessarily require large undertakings. Strive for equity and inclusion instead of equality. In order to develop a fully engaged constituency, individuals must receive *equitable* treatment instead of *equal* treatment. Establishing *equality* means treating everyone the same. *Equity,* in contrast, necessitates transforming the campus community to meet the unique and different needs, interests, and cultural norms of the students, faculty, and staff.

2. **Develop a DEI plan.**

   College leaders should incorporate diversity principles across all business functions and units of the institution. Diversity and equity can lead to inclusion, but inclusion is a value that must be practiced throughout all sectors of the college. Inclusive practices can be integrated into college activities, programs, and services at the college (http://www.diversityjournal.com/1471-moving-from-diversity-to-inclusion). Colleges can consider making diversity principles a curricular requirement for students and a job requirement for employees. College educators should look beyond standard curricular issues to areas such as experiential learning and increased study-abroad opportunities to expose students and employees to further opportunities for education about diversity and cultural competence.

3. Practice broad-based engagement.

College leaders should work to create campus climates that encourage faculty, administrators, and staff members to participate in the development of college-wide policies around diversity, equity, and inclusion. Colleges can create opportunities for interdisciplinary work teams to develop relevant programs and services. The goal is for all employees to demonstrate cultural competence. Community college leaders are encouraged to create a campus climate that embraces contributions from all constituent groups.

4. Conduct professional development training.

Community college leaders must dedicate human and fiscal resources to develop and offer programs that teach cultural competence to all college stakeholders. Building a culture of inclusion requires education through programs that focus on diversity in age, race, religion, culture, social class, gender, sexual orientation, degree of disability, and physical abilities. Professional development training can help employees learn to understand and deal with a wide range of ideas and perspectives in the workplace and in the classroom. Without professional development, the college can be plagued with human relations problems. If employees do not have the skills to deal with diversity, the institution may experience myriad and unnecessary problems. Inside the community college, inclusion practices must be an integral part of the way the college conducts its business. Community college leaders should provide the resources to create an inclusive environment that supports diversity in all respects.

5. Redesign structures, policies, and practices.

The basic structure of a community college affects equity. For example, the community college's intake practices have sorted students according to academic preparation based on placement tests. Evidence from studies on developmental education suggests that such sorting can increase inequalities and inequities in outcomes, particularly as they relate to the attainment of minority and low-income students. Community colleges should review policies and redesign processes, programs, and services to address the diversity of student needs. Diversity, equity, and inclusion must be supported by all sectors of the colleges. Chism (1994) suggested that teachers could provide more meaningful teaching environments by taking student diversity into account. Community college leaders are encouraged to identify ways to understand and embrace the diversity in the student population beyond special events—diversity must be imbedded into the policies and practices at the college. For example, results of studies focusing on effective community colleges reveal the significance of collaboration between academic and student affairs (Jenkins, 2011; Kuh et al., 2005; Muraskin & Lee, 2004). Kuh and colleagues encouraged colleges to examine the importance of student engagement outside the classroom, suggesting that student success requires institutions to provide wide-ranging support services and systematic ways to connect students to those services. In response to the Completion Agenda call for action and reforms in developmental education, some college leaders are now examining the role of academic advisors. According to McCormick (2003), advisors are particularly important in helping students plan their educational program and addressing questions of programs of study and academic pathways. Muraskin and Lee observed that institutions with higher than expected graduation rates have three things in common: (1) high student participation in advising and counseling, (2) intentional academic planning processes, and (3) educational innovations that assist students' learning. It takes all sectors of the college to create optimum teaching and learning environments for students to succeed.

Sustaining Diversity, Equity, and Inclusion

College leaders can make DEI work by focusing their efforts and resources on high-impact areas, especially those that are most relevant to the sustainability of the college's mission. College leaders should routinely and consistently review what their college is doing to inspire transformative thinking about shifting from counting diversity demographics to managing equity and inclusion. Some questions to ask to guide the shifts include:

o How well does your college manage diversity, equity, and inclusion?

o What actions is your college taking to foster an inclusive teaching and learning environment?

o Has your college assessed policies and practices to identify barriers to success for all students?

o How can diversity, equity, and inclusion interventions address gaps and barriers in policies and practices at your institution?

o What are the next steps that your institution must take to improve diversity, equity, and inclusion?

In closing, we believe that college leaders should work collaboratively and within established governance structures to create campus climates that transform the traditional thinking that drives their policies and the allocation of resources. Bauman and colleagues (2005) point out that institutions must make adjustments in programs and services in order to achieve equitable educational outcomes for all students. They argue that institutions have responsibilities for fostering teaching and learning environments to make educational opportunities inclusive for all students. Colleges must make the shift from merely measuring the demographic changes to placing an emphasis on institutional practices to ensure that a diverse population of students and employees receives equitable treatment and a voice in the implementation of the policies and practices that affect them. Sustainability of any diversity, equity, and inclusion initiative happens only when all stakeholders are actively engaged in the design, development, and administration of the diversity and inclusion initiatives.

Issues to Consider

A. Is there a "critical mass" of employees and students that must be realized before a college can truly be considered to be diverse, equitable, and inclusive? What should the percentage be?

B. What are some strategies that colleges could use to attract a more diverse pool of applicants for positions and to employ more applicants from underrepresented groups?

C. What should colleges do to help employees and students from underrepresented groups to feel welcomed and to assist them in being successful?

D. Students at several colleges and universities are demanding that institutions rename buildings and remove statues that honor individuals they consider to be racist. Are these demands reasonable, or are the students asking for too much? How would you respond to such a demand?

Case Scenario

The Diversity Protest

Context

Palomar College is a single-campus, comprehensive community college located in northern San Diego County, California. The college operates from a main campus in San Marcos and several smaller education centers throughout a 2,500-square-mile service area. A five-member elected board of trustees governs the college district with delegated responsibility for administering the college given to a superintendent/ president (CEO). Although the board elections are nonpartisan, the members reflect the very conservative Republican views of the electorate. The president of the Associated Student Government sits at the board table and, as this story begins, does not have a vote.

The CEO is in his eighth year of leadership of the college and, for the last few years, has given direct attention to improving both the quality and diversity of the faculty and staff. Student enrollment has grown during the eight-year tenure of the CEO by 39 percent to 21,500. At the same time, the communities served by the college have become more ethnically diverse. Twenty-six percent of the population served by the college is minority, with the Hispanic population growing significantly. The college has done a good job of providing proportional access to the population: Twenty-nine percent of the students are from minority groups.

On the other hand, employees of the college do not reflect the ethnic makeup of the communities served. During the tenure of the CEO, the percentage of full-time faculty from minority groups had increased from 9 percent to 12 percent; that of administrators had increased from 12 percent to 21 percent; and that of classified support staff had increased from 17 percent to 21 percent. The CEO was just concluding a difficult struggle with faculty to change the employment policies and procedures, requiring sufficient numbers of qualified candidates and sufficient gender and ethnic representation in the applicant, interview, and finalist pools. Under the proposed policy, the CEO would interview the top three or more unranked candidates for each faculty and administrative position and, after meeting with the search committee, would recommend his selection to the board for employment. If at any time the administration felt that the pools did not have sufficient diversity or sufficient numbers of qualified candidates, the search would either be extended or canceled. The CEO could waive these requirements in highly unusual circumstances (e.g., lack of male applicants for nursing faculty positions after evidence of unsuccessful attempts).

The policy and procedure changes that the CEO had sought had, after several months and not without opposition, made it through the college internal governance and were scheduled to appear for information at the next meeting of the board of trustees. However, before the board meeting, the CEO received a letter from the State Chancellor's Office stating that Palomar College had not met a state-mandated goal that 30 percent of new employees in a three-year period should be members of ethnic minority groups. The chancellor notified the CEO that he would be dispatching a Technical Assistance Team to Palomar College, as well as to other colleges in similar circumstances, to review employment policies and practices and to make recommendations to the CEO and the board. Although the CEO saw the review of the Technical Assistance Team to be positive in helping the college to focus on improving policies and practices, conservative local newspapers ran stories that portrayed the visit as punitive.

When the CEO introduced the board agenda item to change the employment policies, board members were influenced by the negative newspaper stories about the scheduled visit of the Technical Assistance Team. The board chair commented that he resented interference by the state. Another trustee, who was a retired faculty member, said that she did not like the emphasis on diversity in the proposed policy, and that Palomar should hire quality not diversity. Their comments were reported in three local newspapers the following day.

The comments from the board members inflamed the minority communities. At the following board meeting, the president of the North County NAACP joined minority faculty members and students in condemning the comments from the two trustees as being insensitive and potentially racist. Despite words of caution from the CEO, the board chair angrily gaveled down a student who called the board racist. The following day, minority students, led by MEChA, the African-American Student Alliance, and the Native American Student Alliance, paraded through the campus with mock coffins for the board chair and the trustee who made the comment about hiring quality rather than diversity. With the encouragement of minority faculty members and community members, the students decided to turn their demonstration into a campout in front of the campus and pitched makeshift tents. The two coffins were predominantly displayed near the tents along Mission Road near the campus entrance.

Local newspapers ran front-page stories on the protest. The CEO received notes from a few faculty members urging him not to cave in to pressure from liberal minorities. A nonminority male student came to the CEO's office saying that he was thinking about organizing a counter protest of White students. The protesters received notes handed to them from passing automobiles, many in support of their efforts. However, one note threatened that they would be shot if they continued their protest. The national head of the White Aryan Resistance, a separatist organization, lives in the college district.

Summary of the Case

The community served by the college is changing demographically, becoming more ethnically diverse. However, the community and its leadership remain very conservative. The CEO has been successful in leading the college through several financial and political challenges during his eight-year tenure. His efforts to bring greater quality and diversity to the faculty and staff have not necessarily been welcomed by faculty and trustees. Trustee comments about proposed policy changes and an impending state Technical Assistance Team visit ignited a student protest and presented the CEO with the need to protect freedom of speech, protect the safety of the student protesters, and keep the situation from escalating further. Three local newspapers are competing for readership. One of the newspapers has assigned the story to a young, aggressive investigative reporter who has interviewed community leaders, students, board members, and the CEO. She is following the story closely. The trustees to whom the CEO reports are under attack by the protesters.

Questions to Consider

1. Should the CEO allow the protesting students to continue their camp-out protest? If so, under what conditions?
2. If the CEO allows the protest to continue, what should he do to ensure the safety and security of the students and the campus?

3. How should the CEO respond to the student who suggested a counter protest?

4. Should the CEO delegate dealing with the student protesters to his vice president for student affairs or to one of his minority administrators?

5. How should the CEO deal with his board members?

6. How should the CEO deal with the press?

7. What, if anything, should the CEO report to the State Chancellor's Office?

Thoughts and Analysis

1. College campuses are historically centers for freedom of speech. If the CEO were to consider a forced end to the demonstrations, he would be acting against his own values and would need legal advice.

2. Classes end at 10:00 p.m. on the San Marcos campus of Palomar College. The campus generally closes at 11:00 p.m., all facilities, including restrooms, are locked, and Campus Security leaves for the evening.

3. With the strong emotions involved on both sides of the diversity issue, and with the head of the national White Aryan Resistance living in the college district, there is a very real threat of violence.

4. Since the protesters are calling for the removal of the board chair and another trustee, the CEO's job security may be at stake.

5. The student protesters have no single authority to represent them, and the Hispanic and African-American students do not always agree, making it difficult to negotiate an agreement to end the protest. The Native American students pulled back from the demonstration.

Outcomes

The CEO decided to allow the minority students to continue their protest. He arranged to keep restrooms near the campsites open throughout the evenings, had water delivered to the students, and assigned 24-hour security to protect the students and the campus. He successfully discouraged the nonminority students from mounting a counter protest by pledging to work on behalf of all students and to seek a peaceful resolution to the protests. The CEO kept law enforcement officials, the trustees, the State Chancellor's Office, and the press informed of developments on a regular basis. He wrote an opinion editorial for the largest of the local newspapers, outlining the college's efforts to improve both the quality and diversity of its faculty and staff. The CEO decided to negotiate with the student protesters directly and at the campsite rather than delegating the responsibility or requiring the students to come to his office. During the 11-day protest, the students and the CEO developed a respectful and trusting relationship.

After the student protesters told the CEO of the threat of a shooting, he ordered the protesters to move their tents to the interior of the campus. The protesters refused to obey the order, saying that they were prepared to sacrifice for the rights of minority students. The CEO told the protestors that he was responsible for their safety and would contact the sheriff's department and have the students arrested if they did not obey. The students responded that the CEO could do what he had to do, and they would do what they had to do. The CEO called the sheriff, and deputies arrived in about a half hour along with the investigative newspaper reporter. The deputy said that he had to hear the students disobey the CEO's order before he would arrest them. The CEO called the students together and again asked them to move their tents to the interior of the campus where they would not be susceptible to a drive-by shooting. The students changed their minds and agreed to do so, ending the standoff and a certain front-page newspaper story.

In the course of the protest, the students presented a list of demands for changes that they felt would improve the climate for diversity at the college. The CEO worked with students, community members, faculty, and trustees to achieve a mutually acceptable resolution to the issues that were raised. Discussions with the protesters were conducted in a respectful and non-confrontational atmosphere. In all of the meetings with the protesters, the CEO affirmed the right to free speech and the college's commitment to increase the diversity of the faculty. Throughout the negotiations, the CEO was focused on ensuring freedom of speech, open discussion of the issues, academic freedom, open communications to all concerned, and the safety and security of the students and the campus.

The protest ended with an agreement on a plan for increasing diversity awareness that included the formation of a task force to address diversity issues, the recommendation for cultural awareness courses for employees and board members, recommendation for an advisory vote for the student trustee, and continuing dialogue between students and administrators. The state Technical Assistance Team's major recommendation to improve the hiring rate of minorities was to give less weight to previous teaching experience when evaluating resumes. The board of trustees approved the CEO's recommended new employment policies unanimously. The CEO was named as an Honorary Elder the following year by the Western Region of the National Council on Black American Affairs.

This case study is reprinted with permission from the League for Innovation in the Community College (Originally published by George R. Boggs in L. W. Tyree & M. D. Milliron (Eds.) *Leadership Dialogues: Community College Case Studies to Consider, League for Innovation in the Community College*. Phoenix, AZ, pp. 119–122, 2004.

REFERENCES

Aguirre, A. Jr. (2000). *Women and Minority Faculty in the Academic Workplace: Recruitment, Retention, and Academic Culture* (ASHE-ERIC Higher Education Report). San Francisco, CA: Jossey-Bass.

American Association of Community Colleges. (2014). *Empowering Community Colleges to Build the Nation's Future: An Implementation Guide*. Washington, DC: Author. Retrieved from http://www.aacc21stcentury center.org/wp-content/uploads/2014/04/EmpoweringCommunityColleges_final.pdf.

American Council on Education. (2002). Amicus Briefs: *Grutter v. Bollinger* and *Gratz v Bollinger*. Retrieved from http://www.acenet.edu/news-room/Pages/Amicus-Brief-Supreme-Court-Michigan-Admissions-Cases.aspx.

American Council on Education (2015). Amicus Briefs: *Fisher v. University of Texas*. Retrieved from http://www.acenet.edu/news-room/Pages/Resources-Fisher-v-University-of-Texas-at-Austin-Before-the-US-Supreme-Court.aspx.

American Council on Education (2013). Legal Update: *Schutte v. Coalition to Defend Affirmative Action*. Retrieved from http://www.acenet.edu/news-room/Pages/Legal-Update-Schuette-v-Coalition-to-Defend-Affirmative-Action.aspx.

Bailey, T., & Morest, V. S. (2006). *Defending the Community College Equity Agenda.* Baltimore, MD: Johns Hopkins University Press.

Barr, R. B., & Tagg, J. (1995, November/December). From Teaching to Learning: A New Paradigm for Undergraduate Education. *Change, 6,* 13–25.

Bauman, G., Bustillos, L. T., Bensimon, E. M., Brown, C. M. II, & Bartee, R. D. (2005). *Achieving Equitable Educational Outcomes with All Students: The Institution's Roles and Responsibilities.* In Making Excellence Inclusive: Preparing Students for an Era of Greater Expectations. Washington, DC: Association of American Colleges and Universities.

Bensimon, E. M, & Polkinghorne, D. (2003). *Why Equity Matters: Implications for a Democracy.* Los Angeles: University of Southern California Rossier School of Education, Center for Urban Education.

Border, L. B., & Chism, N. V. (Eds.). (1992). Teaching for Diversity. *New Directions for Teaching and Learning* (No. 49). San Francisco, CA: Jossey-Bass.

Bush, E. C., & Bush, L. (2010). Calling Out the Elephant: An Examination of African American Male Achievement in Community College. *Journal of African American Males in Education* 1(1), 40–62. Retrieved from https://interwork.sdsu.edu/sp/m2c3/files/2012/10/Calling-Out-the-Elephant.pdf.

Cabrera, A. F., Nora, A., Terenzini, P. T., Pascarella, E., & Hagedorn, L. S. (1999). Campus Racial Climate and the Adjustment of Students to College: A Comparison between White Students and African American Students. *Journal of Higher Education, 70*(2), 134–160.

Chang, M. J. (2000). Improving Campus Racial Dynamics: A Balancing Act Among Competing Interests. *Review of Higher Education, 23*(2), 153–175.

Chism, N. (1994). Taking Student Diversity into Account. In W. J. McKeachie (Ed.), *Teaching Tips: Strategies, Research, and Theory for College and University Teachers* (9th ed., pp. 223–237). Lexington, MA: D.C. Heath.

Cohen, A. M., & Brawer, F. B. (1996). *The American Community College.* San Francisco, CA: Jossey-Bass.

Center for Community College Student Engagement. (2015). *Aspirations to Achievement: Men of Color and Community Colleges.* Retrieved from http://www.ccsse.org/center/initiatives/moc/special.cfm.

Davis, B. G. (2009). Learning Styles and Preferences. *Tools for Teaching* (pp. 75–76). San Francisco, CA: Jossey-Bass.

Dougherty, K. J., & Kienzl, G. (2006). It's Not Enough to Get Through the Open Door: Inequalities by Social Background in Transfer from Community Colleges to Four-Year Colleges. *Teachers' College Record, 108,* 452–487.

Evans, N. J., Forney, D. S., & Guido-DiBrito, F. (1998). Gay, Lesbian, and Bisexual Development. In *Student Development in College: Theory, Research, and Practice* (pp. 113–116). San Francisco, CA: Jossey-Bass.

Goebel, B. A. (1995). "Who Are All These People?": Some Pedagogical Implications of Diversity in the Multicultural Classroom. In B. A. Goebel & J. C. Hall (Eds.), *Teaching a "New Canon": Students, Teachers, and Texts in the College Literature Classroom* (pp. 22–31). Urbana, IL: National Council of Teachers of English.

Goodwin, B., & Miller, K. (2013). Research Says/Evidence on Flipped Classrooms Is Still Coming In. *Technology-Rich Learning, 70*(6), 78–80, 149. Retrieved from http://bit.ly/1clfxgX.

Grodsky, E., & Kurlaender, M. (2010). *Equal Opportunity in Higher Education: The Past and Future of Proposition 209.* Cambridge, MA: Harvard Education Press.

Harper, S. R. (2009). Race, Interest Convergence, and Transfer Outcomes for Black Male Student Athletes. *New Directions for Community Colleges* (No. 147), 29–37.

Harper, S. R., & Harris III, F. (2012). *A Role for Policymakers in Improving the Status of Black Male Students in U.S. Higher Education.* Washington DC: Institute for Higher Education Policy.

Harris III, F., & Wood, J. L. (2013). Student Success for Men of Color in Community Colleges: A Review of Published Literature and Research, 1998-2012. *Journal of Diversity in Higher Education, 6*(3), 174–185.

Heilman, M. E. (2001). Description and Prescription: How Gender Stereotypes Prevent Women's Ascent up the Organizational Ladder. *Journal of Social Issues, 57*(4), 657–674.

Hurtado, S. (2007). Linking Diversity with the Educational and Civic Missions of Higher Education. *Review of Higher Education, 30*(2), 185–196.

Jenkins, D. (2011, April). Get with the Program: Accelerating Community College Students' Entry into and Completion of Programs of Study. (CCRC Working Paper No. 32). New York, NY: Community College Research Center, Teachers College, Columbia University.

Jordan, P. G. (2008) African-American Male Students' Success in an Urban Community College: A Case Study. Dissertations available from ProQuest. Paper AAI3311541.

Kuh, G., Kinzie, J., Schuh, J., & Whitt, E. (1991). *Involving Colleges: Successful Approaches to Fostering Student Learning and Development Outside the Classroom.* San Francisco, CA: Jossey-Bass.

Kuh, G. D., Kinzie, J., Schuh, J. H., & Whitt, E. J. (2005). *Assessing Conditions for Student Success: An Inventory to Enhance Educational Effectiveness.* San Francisco: Jossey-Bass.

Lang, W. A., Harriett, B. D., & Cadet, M. (2013). *Completing the Mission II: A Study of Veteran Students' Progress Toward Degree Attainment in the Post 9/11 Era.* Pat Tillman Foundation and Operation College Promise.

Retrieved from http://www.ccmountainwest.org/sites/default/files/
completing_mission_ii.pdf.

McBain, L., Kim, Y. M., Cook, B., & Snead, K. (2012). *Soldier to Student*
[Assessing Campus Programs for Veterans and Service Members].
Washington, DC: American Council on Education.

McCormick, A. (2003). Swirling and Double-Dipping: New Patterns of Student
Attendance and their Implications for Higher Education. *New Directions
for Higher Education* (No. 121), 13–24.

McPhail, I. P., & McPhail, C. J. (1999). Transforming Classroom Practice for
African-American Learners: Implication for the Learning Paradigm. In
Removing Vestiges: Research-Based Strategies to Promote Inclusion
(No. 2 pp. 25–35). Anapolis Junction, MD: Community College Press.

McPhail, I. P., McPhail, C. J., & Smilkstein, R., (2001). Culture, Style, and
Cognition Expanding the Boundaries of the Learning Paradigm for
African-American Learners in the Community College. Retrieved from
http://www.eric.ed.gov/contentdelivery/servlet/ERICServlet?accno=ED455855.

Moody, J. (2004). Supporting Women and Minority Faculty. *Academe*
90(1), 47–52.

Moore, W. (2006). *Behind the Open Door: Racism and Other Contradictions
in the Community College*. Bloomington, IN: Trafford Publishing.

Muraskin, L., & Lee, J. (2004, December). *Raising the Graduation Rates
of Low-Income College Students*. The Pell Institute for the Study of
Opportunity in Higher Education. http://www.pellinstitute.org/gradrates/
Pell_Web.pdf.

Pettigrew, T. F. (1994). Prejudice and Discrimination on the College Campus.
In J. L. Eberhardt & S. E. Fiske (Eds.), *Confronting Racism: The Problem
and the Response* (pp. 263–279). Thousand Oaks, CA: Sage.

Rankin, S. R. (2003). *Campus Climate for Gay, Lesbian, Bisexual, and Transgender
People: A National Perspective*. New York, NY: The National Gay and
Lesbian Task Force Policy Institute. Retrieved from: http://www.ngltf.org.

Russa, D. J. (2007). Self-Determination and Success Outcomes of Two-Year
College Students with Disabilities. *Journal of College Reading and
Learning, 37*(2), 26–46.

Sanlo, R. L. (Ed.). (1998). *Working with Lesbian, Gay, Bisexual, and
Transgender College Students: A Handbook for faculty and Administrators*.
Westport, CT: Greenwood. (ED 427 802)

Smith, D. G. (2000). How to Diversify the Faculty. *Academe, 86*(5) Retrieved
from http://www.aaup.org/publications/Academe/2000/00so/
SO00Smit.htm.

Slaughter, J. (2004, November 1). *Diversity and Equity in Higher Education:
A New Paradigm for Institutional Excellence*. Major address at

National Association of State Universities and Land Grant Colleges
(Now the Association of Public and Land Grant Universities), June 23,
2003. Washington, DC. Retrieved from http://.web.jhu.edu.

Treisman, P. U. (1992). Studying Students Studying Calculus: A Look at the
Lives of Minority Mathematics Students in College. *College Math Journal*,
23(5), 362–373.

Trower, C. A., & Chait, R. P. (2002). Faculty Diversity: Too Little for Too Long.
Harvard Magazine Online. Retrieved from http://www.harvard- magazine
.com/on-line/030218.html.

Tyson, C. (2014, August 21). Ferguson's College Refuge. *Inside Higher Education*.
https://www.insidehighered.com/news/2014/08/21/community-college-
serves-ferguson-mo-has-high-aspirations-low-graduation-rates.

White House (2014). *My Brother's Keeper*. Retrieved June 2, 2015, from: http://
www.whitehouse.gov/my-brothers-keeper.

6

GOVERNANCE, COMMUNICATION, AND MEDIA RELATIONS

Trustees

Discussions of community college governance issues start with those who serve to represent the owners of the colleges to oversee them and to set their policies. In the case of public community colleges, the owners are the members of the public who pay for the development, maintenance, and operations of the colleges, and the representatives are the boards of governors or boards of trustees. Community college CEOs—presidents, superintendent/presidents, or chancellors—consistently rate developing and maintaining positive and productive relationships with their boards as one of the most important but challenging aspects of their jobs (Boggs, 2006). Positive relationships between boards and CEOs do not happen accidentally; they must be nourished and developed. From a broader perspective, the real challenge for CEOs who report to college or district governing boards is to assist their boards in becoming as effective as they can be.

Whether trustees are elected or appointed depends upon state policy. In some states, a state board governs the system of community colleges or even the entire state system of higher education. Some states have a combination of a state board and local boards of trustees. The authority of the local board can be constrained by acts of the state legislature or the state board. In some cases, local boards are merely advisory and cannot set policy. Where trustees are appointed, the appointing authority can be the state governor or elected local officials. Sometimes the appointments are made by a specified combination of officials. There is no clear evidence that appointed or elected boards or state or local boards are more effective or less political in their actions.

Community college boards are responsible for the current and future vitality of the institutions that are central to educational opportunity for individuals and to the economic health of communities. The members are entrusted by the appointing body or the electorate to ensure that the college or district is operated effectively, efficiently, and ethically; that it is responsive to the educational and economic development needs of the community; and that planning is done so the college can effectively serve future generations. The role of trustees is to govern and not to administer the college nor to draft the plans for its future. However, they are to see that these responsibilities are met and to monitor the progress of the college.

The board should delegate the administration of the college and its internal governance and planning processes to its CEO. The relationship between a board and its CEO is an important one; neither can be very effective unless both are. It is essential that the expectations for both the CEO and the board are clear and that communications are regular and open. The CEO's office must be the main point of contact between the board and the college staff. Board members should be informed about important problems, events, or issues before they hear about them from outside sources or before they are asked to respond to the press. CEOs should not try to protect board members from problems; instead, they should protect them from surprises. All trustees should receive the same information. No board member should be placed at a disadvantage by not having needed information.

Trustees need to be informed to do their jobs. However, it is a mistake to overwhelm board members with unnecessary information. CEOs should assist trustees to focus on the most important information they need to make policy decisions, to monitor the implementation of those policies, and to assess the progress of the college in meeting the goals established by the board. Initiatives such as Achieving the Dream have served to focus boards on important college outcomes and the progress that the institution is making to improve them. The Association of Community College Trustees (ACCT) sponsors a Governance Institute for Student Success, which is focused on board responsibilities for student outcomes. Closing achievement gaps and improving course and program completion rates for students are among the most significant issues facing colleges today, and boards should have the information they need through data dashboards or reports so they can establish realistic goals and monitor progress.

Board agenda items may seem to provide an opportunity to make isolated and unrelated decisions. However, it is important that the actions of the board fit into the overall goals of the college. It is often helpful for the board and the CEO to schedule occasional retreats and workshops. At these meetings, away from the demands of regular board meetings, trustees and the CEO can set goals for themselves, evaluate their progress in meeting these goals, and assess the progress of the college toward their vision of the future. Boards should expect their CEOs to identify and suggest goals as well as to provide information on goal achievement.

Boards have a special responsibility for future generations of students. While the college staff may be focused on short-term problems, trustees have an obligation to insist on long-term planning. Here again, it is not the responsibility of the board to draw up long-range plans, but to insist that the administration, faculty, and staff do so in terms the board can approve.

Trustees and CEOs, of course, are human and subject to the full range of emotions, political pressures, interests, and reactions that can be observed in any group of people. It is important to remember, however, that this group is a very visible one. The behavioral dynamics between the board and CEO and among trustees have an effect throughout the college and often into the community. Positive and productive relationships set a very positive tone for everyone at the college. However, reports of "split boards," CEO–board problems, or "rogue trustees" and the damage they cause to colleges extend beyond local communities and often make national news.

Terry O'Banion (2009) has written about how disruptive some trustees can be for colleges. His survey of community college CEOs indicated that these "rogue trustees" were prevalent and that they consumed an inordinate amount of staff and meeting time, often violating codes of conduct and placing their own special interests over the interests of the college. Dealing with this kind of disruption can be a significant challenge for board chairs, CEOs, and the entire college community.

CEOs should work with their board chairs to try to heal divisions on the board. Board decisions should be made upon the merits of the issue and not upon preconceived positions of factions or individuals. Since trustees bring a variety of perspectives to their roles, it may not always be possible, even after thorough discussion, to reach consensus on every issue. In such cases, the CEO should help the board to respect the minority opinion but support the decision of the majority. The board and the CEO must move on to the next issue without being influenced by hard feelings from a previous decision. Trustees deserve the thoughtful advice of their CEO on every important action. High ethical principles must guide both the CEO and the board in all they do.

In cases in which a CEO has to work with a consistently split board, it is important that the CEO not become politically aligned with one faction over another. Political winds change, and a majority faction might find itself in the minority after the next election or appointment. These political shifts can trap a CEO and damage or end an otherwise successful career. Political turmoil among trustees or between the CEO and the board is not healthy for any college.

Every person has special interests, and most of us belong to groups that advocate for certain values, ideals, or political or religious beliefs. Some board members or their relatives may be employed by businesses that are potential contractors with the college. However, neither trustees nor CEOs should use their positions to place any special interest above the interest of the college. Even the appearance of a conflict can create negative publicity and perhaps legal problems for the college and the individuals involved.

Board members and their CEOs must recognize that deliberations and discussions of the board, staff, and legal counsel in closed or executive session are not to be released or discussed in public without prior approval of the board by majority vote. Open-meeting laws in most states restrict closed-session topics to such items as personnel matters, student discipline, pending litigation, employee negotiations, and land acquisition. Disclosure of confidential information is not only unethical; it may result in costly litigation against the college and the individuals involved.

Today's most effective college leaders facilitate the participation of people in making the decisions that will affect them. Faculty, staff members, students, and community members often serve on advisory or participatory governance committees. Because of the size and complexity of the organization, CEOs will have to delegate many decisions to others. Neither the delegation nor the participation of others, however, relieves the CEO or the board from responsibility for proper administration and governance of the college. The CEO and the board must retain the right to send a recommendation back to a committee or an administrator for further consideration or to make a decision different from the one recommended.

Smaller boards (nine members or less) most commonly found in public community colleges can usually operate as a committee of the whole and often do not need to divide into trustee committees. However, smaller boards may ask nontrustee community advisory committees or internal college committees to provide recommendations as a way of including more points of view before the board is required to act. Where board committees are a part of the structure of the board, CEOs and their staffs generally provide support and advice for committee work. They have the responsibility to help develop committee agendas that focus on policies and evaluation of progress. CEOs may have to caution board members to avoid getting too specialized and concerned about one aspect of the college at the expense of the entire institution. If board committees exist, they are to advise the board, not college staff members. CEOs must guard against the risk that smaller boards and standing committees of larger boards will drift away from policy issues into administrative decisions. For boards that operate with a committee structure, the roles and responsibilities of the committees should be a part of every board orientation and every board evaluation.

If the board has more than ten members, it may be difficult to create an environment that allows the trustees to deliberate on the issues and to feel personally involved. Meetings are usually infrequent because they are more difficult to schedule. There is a danger that the executive committee of a large board will take over the responsibilities of the board. At the same time, critics of small boards say that they fail to reflect a sufficient variety of perspectives and therefore lack the depth necessary to deal wisely with the issues confronting the college.

Although college CEOs cannot determine the size of the board, they can mitigate some of the potential problems with boards that are either very large or very small. Through an appropriate committee structure—and with proper precautions and consistent reminders about appropriate responsibilities from the CEO—it is usually possible to divide large boards into a suitable number of smaller groups in which the members are actively involved and able to deliberate appropriately.

Although the board is responsible for its own meeting preparation and conduct, the technical task of preparing the agenda for board meetings is an important responsibility for the college CEO. The agendas should address board priorities that the CEO and trustees develop over time, perhaps emanating from study sessions or retreats, and not just be a collection of routine approval actions. In colleges that have strong board chairs, the chair may also be involved in the development of the agenda. Most of the work of preparing the agenda and gathering the backup materials is done by the members of the CEO's executive leadership team and coordinated by the CEO's staff. It is important to get the materials put together and distributed in time to meet the legal requirements for public notification and to allow the board members time to review and study the issues.

Trustees and the CEO should welcome and encourage the orderly involvement of students, employees, and citizens of the district when discussing agenda items. Their views should be considered by the board in its deliberations. The board should also set aside time on the agenda for public comment during the meeting. Alternately, public comments regarding agenda items may be heard as the board takes up these items. Some board policies require individuals to submit written requests to the CEO before addressing the board. Policies may also place time limits on individual statements. CEOs and boards can use these policies to control the meetings, but they must be careful not to restrict public comment. In order to avoid violating both the public trust and open meeting laws, board members should not engage in lengthy discussions or make decisions about items not on the agenda.

Board agenda items may seem to provide an opportunity to take isolated and unrelated actions. However, it is important for the actions of the board to fit into the overall mission and long-range goals of the college. Board retreats or planning meetings give the board members an opportunity to think about the big picture, and CEOs should use these occasions to help trustees to understand how their actions at board meetings move the college toward its vision.

Board members set policy acting as a unit and based in large part upon the information they receive in board agendas and meetings. Although conventional wisdom is that policy development is the prerogative of the board and administering those policies is the business of the CEO and the staff, in practice trustees usually expect their CEO to recommend policies for board approval. Because the board relies on the CEO to implement its policies, trustees cannot effectively set policy in isolation from the CEO and the staff. Board members need to be briefed on how policy recommendations are brought to their attention. In colleges that have strong traditions of faculty and staff participation, recommendations for changes in policy are studied thoroughly by internal committees and constituencies before they are brought to the board. The CEO should be prepared to make a recommendation on proposed policy changes in every case. When the CEO recommends that the board take action on an agenda item, it usually has the benefit of hours of work on the part of the college professional staff. Board members should be cautioned against taking action on items that are brought to their attention by special interests and that have not gone through review by college staff and the CEO. CEOs should introduce recommendations for board action by including information about the process used to bring the recommendation to them, the reasons for the action, pertinent data, impact on the college and the community, implications for student learning, fiscal implications, and information about any related laws and current policies.

CEOs have an obligation to inform the board regularly on the implementation of policies. These reports to the board focus the board appropriately on policies and their implementation; they are used to monitor or gauge the degree to which previous board directions on policy have been satisfied. These reports should provide information about performance against preestablished and agreed-upon criteria, and they should be systematically provided to the board. A data-informed institutional effectiveness program that reports on benchmarks and progress toward institutional goals can be the basis for a good monitoring system. It should be designed by the CEO and staff and based upon board priorities.

Careful attention to monitoring reports is very important for boards to be sure that the college is fulfilling its mission. Summaries of accreditation reports and state board reports can provide useful information about college performance. The reports of outside auditing firms provide valuable information about the college's financial operations, investment strategies, and fiscal solvency.

CEOs must help boards to recognize the complexity of the college and its operations, taking the long-range view, especially when the internal college community may be reluctant to do so. Boards should periodically review the college mission and vision statements. They and their CEOs must be sure that the college community engages in planning and develops a useful educational master plan in agreement with the college mission and vision statements. The facility, staff, instruction, student services, and information technology plans must be integral parts of the educational master plan for the college. CEOs can also involve trustees early in this process by engaging the board in a discussion about community needs.

While the internal college community is often focused on short-term problems, trustees and CEOs have an obligation to insist on long-term planning. Because colleges are human service institutions, they tend to focus on the problems of its people and can lose sight of facility needs. Here again, it is not the responsibility of the board or the CEO to draw up the long-range plans, but to insist that the administration, faculty, and staff do so in terms that the board can approve. By developing a calendar for the development or periodic review and board approval of the long-range plan, the CEO can help the board to meet this important responsibility.

Some states have passed laws that add a student to the membership of the college board of trustees. Many legislators have put students on boards believing that that their presence at the board table will ensure that the board listens to the views of students while making its deliberations. Student trustees are usually elected by the students at large and have the obligation to represent student perspectives to the board and to report and perhaps explain board action to the student government. Student trustees usually do not have the same rights and responsibilities as publicly elected or politically appointed board members. Sometimes they are given an advisory vote, but they usually cannot make or second motions, and, in some states, they may not be allowed to join the board in closed or executive sessions. Nonetheless, the wise CEO will treat the student–trustee relationship with respect and work to develop trustee competencies in the student trustee. The CEO's office, rather than the student affairs office, should be the point of contact for the student trustee, just as it is for the other trustees.

The CEO's office should be the main point of contact between the board and the college. Having a separate board office on a campus or hiring a separate staff for the board threatens the effectiveness of the CEO and invites the board to cross the line between governance and administration. Board members may choose to visit a campus occasionally to become better informed by talking with students and employees and sitting in on some classes and faculty and staff committee meetings. In these cases, the college CEO can facilitate the visit and should always be informed prior to the visit. A trustee who does not inform the CEO about campus visits can, by this action, convey a lack of trust in the CEO. Meetings between a union and a board member during a collective bargaining impasse can damage the negotiations process. A board member who consistently attends internal college committee meetings runs the risk of inhibiting discussion and interfering with a process which is intended to bring informed recommendations to the board.

Media Relations

Most of the nation's community colleges are publicly owned and governed by either elected or appointed trustees. But perhaps the most important link to the public is through the media (newspapers, television, radio, and social media). The media itself is rarely an issue for leadership, but it can have an effect on how significant an issue will be. It is wise for leaders to make media relations a priority. In fact, Fisher and Koch (1996) make the point that the media can make or break a president. The authors wrote:

> The president's off-campus image is composed of a jumble of impressions formed by a relatively inattentive public. However, this image is the major factor in developing a public presence and an aura of

charisma. In the great majority of cases, print and broadcast media (and especially television) are the prime instruments for creating an image. Play these forums as a virtuoso plays violin, although, like most virtuosos, you may seldom be satisfied with the reviews. A direct connection will not always exist between your public image at any moment and the immediate response you wish to receive, but the general public's prevailing impression of a president's standing will set the tone and determine the limits of what faculty, students, staff, alumni, trustees, politicians, public figures, bureaucrats, and potential benefactors will do for the president. Even the most experienced, important, and sophisticated people make judgments based on how many people admire an individual. (Fisher and Koch, 1996, p. 193)

Leaders also need to remember the admonition of Mark Twain, "Never pick a fight with people who buy ink by the barrel." Leaders should strive to develop and maintain a positive and respectful relationship with the media. Too often we have seen college leaders portrayed in a negative light. When that happens, the leader is sometimes helpless to respond appropriately to a tidal wave of media criticism (Carroll, 2004). If the leader responds without a strategy, it usually exacerbates the problem.

One of AACC 's core leadership competencies is the capacity to build and leverage networks and partnerships to advance the mission, vision, and goals of the college. Certainly, a key partnership that community college leaders must develop is one with the local media, and it should be developed strategically. It is important for leaders to develop a media relations strategy based upon what they want to achieve from the media rather than randomly calling reporters when they need coverage or responding to a crisis. Components of an effective media relations strategy include the following actions:

1. **Identify a Spokesperson.** Trustees and college leaders need to determine who can speak for the college in the event of a crisis or difficult issue. The media will usually exploit any differences in accounts or opinions in a story about a crisis or difficult issue, so consistency of message is important.

2. **Be Proactive.** Leaders should get to know editors of local newspapers before a crisis occurs. Bring positive stories to the attention of the media. Include human interest stories about students, faculty, and staff. Reporters appreciate receiving tips to develop their own stories, but they need advance notice of an event in order to do so. When you know of an anticipated

announcement or event, give the media a "heads-up" so reporters have adequate time to prepare.

Although it may seem counterintuitive, it is usually a good idea to inform the media of a negative story rather than risk its discovery from another source. This gives college leaders the opportunity to frame the story accurately. As an example, George Boggs, as a college president, discovered through an anonymous tip and a follow-up audit that the director of the college's food services had embezzled thousands of dollars from the profits of sales. After an investigation to confirm guilt, he informed law enforcement and terminated the director's employment with the college. A press release was issued, and the local newspapers printed the story in inside pages. There were no follow-up stories. An issue that could have been front-page news for an investigative reporter turned out to be a minor issue with no lasting consequence for the college.

3. **Be Available and Responsive.** Leaders should never say, "No comment," when asked a question. Coombs (1998) discussed the importance of understanding the situation and developing responses based on an analytic framework for crisis situations. If something has to be confidential, provide the reasons that it has to be. Be mindful that the motivation of the press is to get a story written by the deadline. Leaders should get back to reporters with responses to their questions as soon as possible. If a leader needs some time to gather information, ask the reporter what his or her deadline is and try to meet it. The media's ability to reach a leader when needed is critical to establishing the leader's image as a reliable face of the college.

4. **Avoid Speaking off the Record.** Leaders need to be cautious about providing information that they do not want to see in print or that they do not want to see attributed to them.

5. **Use the Institution's Website.** Leaders should use their college's websites to communicate to the media. Many leaders overlook the importance of having a media-responsive website. It is wise for leaders to post a media link on the college's home page that shows the name, email, and telephone number of at least one media contact person.

6. **Train Front-Line Employees.** Leaders are encouraged to train college employees who may have to deal with media inquiries.

This includes receptionists, athletic department staff, safety and security personnel, and others who need to know how to direct calls from the media. Key personnel should be trained on how to respond to the press in a positive and friendly manner, but all employees need to know that only designated individuals can speak for the college.

7. **Become the Local Higher Education Authority.** Community college leaders need to do a better job of serving as an information resource to the media on key education issues. One way is for leaders to provide updates to the media on major community college issues along with information about their local community colleges. The leader can also identify experts on the campus who can respond to commonly requested facts about newsworthy issues. Leaders should consider writing opinion editorials on significant educational and social issues for local newspapers.

Despite the best media relations strategies, crises can develop, subjecting the leader and the college to negative media coverage. When these situations happen, electronic media can spread negativity even before the average leader can make a single telephone call. Leaks to the media can come from a disgruntled employee, trustee, administrator, or student. Sometimes sensitive college decisions can create situations that reach a reporter's ear. When the college receives negative coverage, leaders should respond as quickly and as accurately as possible. It is important to own up to any problems and begin to restore confidence in the college (Cohen, 1999). Cohen (1999) noted that an apology often helps restore a damaged relationship between the college and the internal or external community.

Throughout a media relations conflict, the leader must be available to talk as openly as possible with the media and to employees. Leaders who are not responsive or who respond with "No comment" appear to have something to hide. It sends the message that the institution is in the wrong, and it invites reporters to keep digging until they find something— or make it up (Dean, 2004). Coombs and Holladay (2004) pointed out the benefits of "reasoned action" in a crisis communication. They noted that an organization's past affects the reputational threat posed by a crisis when it results from intentional acts by the organization. Coombs and Holladay's Situational Crisis Communication Theory (SCCT) provides a mechanism for anticipating how stakeholders will react to a crisis in terms of the reputational threat posed by the crisis (2004).

Communication is an important key to both building media relationships and solving the media relations problem.

Barnes and Lescault (2011) noted that higher education institutions are now experimenting and evaluating social media as a communication tool with their constituencies. Though much has been written about social media in the business field, and many community colleges have developed social media policies, there is a scarcity of information on how those policies are governed and the leader's role in the media governance process. Michael Ansaldo (2015), a veteran consumer and small-business technology journalist with *PCWorld*, defined a social media governance model as follows:

> A collection of policies, procedures, and educational resources that allow you to manage social media internally. A sound social media governance model empowers your employees while keeping them accountable. It allows you to quickly recover from a blow to your brand, or even sidestep it completely. It helps you keep your social initiatives on track and aligned with your business' strategic goals.

Ansaldo's (2015) media governance model consists of five components: 1) a social media policy that is designed to guide employees and to protect the institution, 2) training that is designed to educate employees how to represent the organization on the social web, 3) monitoring everything from shaping consumer sentiment about the institution's brand to heading off a potential PR crisis, 4) a crisis management plan that outlines how the social media channels can be accessed to deliver a quick and appropriate response, and 5) frequent updates. The leader should designate a social media governance team and a timeline for periodic evaluation of all elements of the social media governance model to assure it's never outdated. Leaders must be mindful that while they have the responsibility for ensuring that the institution's social media policy defines how employees use social media, they must also define their role in the governance of those policies (Ansaldo, 2015).

Zaiontz and Stoner (2015), in #*Follow the Leader: Lessons in Social Media from #Higher Education CEO,* pointed out that college and university presidents are increasingly using social media such as Twitter and Facebook to engage both internal and external constituents. Zaiontz's study confirmed the findings from 2013 Pew Research Center surveys (Parker, Lenhart, & Moor, 2011) that showed that leaders of the nation's colleges and universities are generally a tech-savvy group. The report illustrated that nearly nine in ten (87 percent) use a smartphone daily,

83 percent use a desktop computer, and 65 percent use a laptop. Based on the Pew Research, presidents are ahead of the curve on some of the newer digital technologies: fully half (49 percent) use a tablet computer such as an iPad at least occasionally, and 42 percent use an e-reader such as a Kindle or Nook. The surveys also showed that roughly one-third of college presidents (32 percent) report that they use Facebook weekly or more often; 18 percent say they use Twitter at least occasionally. Presidents can, and do, make significant progress for their institutions through reaching out via social media.

Davis, Deil-Amen, and Canché, (2011), researchers at Claremont Graduate School, found that a relatively low proportion of community college leaders reported that they never use social media for personal (8 percent) or professional (11 percent) purposes. Surprisingly, among those leaders who use social media daily, a higher proportion of them used it for personal (40 percent) rather than for professional (24 percent) purposes. The researchers provided a set of recommendations for community college leaders as they continue to think of purposeful ways to integrate social media into the fabric of their educational institutions. These recommendations include (1) have a strategic plan, (2) get buy-in from executive leadership, faculty, and staff about the importance of social media, (3) think about your resources, (4) add value by using social media applications and other social media platforms, (5) maintain privacy and confidentiality, and (6) define your metrics to assess the effectiveness of social media.

It is clear from the research and our engagement with community college leaders that they are using social media to connect with each other and share information and ideas (Solis, 2008). Through the use of social media, some community colleges leaders are reshaping their leadership platforms to connect with and inform constituent groups. Indeed, community college leaders are in some ways redefining leadership though their varied use of social media.

Delegation and Internal Governance

A community college CEO, through authority delegated by the board of trustees, is responsible for the effective and efficient administration of the college and is expected to recommend policies and policy changes to the board and to develop and revise the administrative procedures to implement them. Likewise, the CEO must delegate certain administrative responsibilities to senior administrators. To carry out these responsibilities in a collegial setting, it is important that avenues are established to advise the CEO and senior administrators with regard to both operations and the development or revision of polices and procedures. College and campus committees are the most common avenues for the CEO and senior administrators to gather advice from those who are expected to implement decisions and policies.

Administrative committees serve two purposes. They provide advice to a particular administrator in the area of operations. They also serve as a communication vehicle to ensure that procedures are interpreted and applied in a uniform manner. Generally, administrative committees are made up of those who report to the administrator who chairs the committee. Agendas can include confidential and sensitive items. A president's or chancellor's cabinet is an example of an administrative committee.

Participatory (sometimes call *shared*) *governance committees* differ from administrative committees in that they bring together representatives of the college's constituent groups. They provide an avenue for an administrator to receive valuable advice from those who are most knowledgeable about specific aspects of the college or district while also providing an opportunity for employees and students to have a say in recommendations that will affect them. Recommendations for new policies and procedures or for changes in policies and procedures are best brought before a governance committee before being forwarded to the CEO or the board for action. Generally, governance committees are made up of a specific number of representatives either appointed or nominated by the constituent groups. Employee unions, as collective bargaining groups with special legal status, are not usually considered constituent groups for the purpose of participatory governance.

Sometimes, internal governance processes become ineffective or overly bureaucratic. College practices that are hindrances to effective management or the ability to serve students and communities may develop over time and may even be memorialized in union contracts. When colleges operate in a union environment, changes in practices often need to be negotiated.

When internal governance practices become ineffective, faculty, staff, and administrators can be frustrated by how long it takes to make decisions. Communication mechanisms can break down, leaving people uninformed about the disposition of recommendations that were forwarded to committees. When committee members come to believe that decisions are made by majority vote, administrators may not know the extent of their authority and how they will be held accountable for decisions and their implementation.

Bowen and Tobin (2015) argue that interpretations of shared governance are the major reasons that vertical modes of decision making in the academy, focused on departmental authority, are not flexible and responsive enough even when dealing with academic and professional matters. They make the case that current models have to give way to more horizontal ways of organizing discussion of new approaches to teaching and learning. Carefully considered arrangements for broader sharing of perspectives, cutting across departmental lines, have become more essential. But Bowen and Tobin make it clear that their suggested changes should not be interpreted as an endorsement of shared final decision-making authority, which, they say, needs to be located unambiguously in the hands of senior administrators who have campus-, university-, and sector-wide perspectives and who can be—and should be—held accountable for their decisions.

Academic Senates

Most institutions of higher education, including community colleges, have academic or faculty senates with the primary focus on academic and professional matters, such as curriculum, grading policies, degree requirements, student learning and success strategies, accreditation requirements and standards, faculty qualifications, and faculty professional development and training.

In California, academic senates have been written into the law. Community college reform legislation, passed in 1988, requires college boards and CEOs to consult collegially with academic senates and to seek active participation of other constituents such as classified staff or students in appropriate areas. The state board of governors defined the term "consult collegially" to mean either to rely primarily on the advice and judgment of the academic senate in academic and professional areas or to reach mutual agreement with the academic senate in these areas.

Search Committees

There is perhaps no other decision that is as important in shaping the culture of a college than who gets hired. Search committees must be properly oriented and trained, not only to ensure that the candidates they forward best meet the needs of the college, but also to treat all applicants fairly and to avoid costly legal problems. Search committees should receive training in affirmative action and the legalities of interviews. An administrator and an affirmative action representative should be present during all interviews conducted by search committees. A seemingly innocent but illegal or inappropriate question of an applicant could easily lead to a big problem for the college. A breach of confidentiality could damage the career of a candidate and likewise lead to a lawsuit.

Search committees should not be led to believe that they would make the hiring decision; they should recommend an agreed-upon number of qualified finalists to the appropriate administrator. If an administrator does not approve of any of the finalists forwarded by a search committee, the administrator should be able to ask the search committee to forward additional names or to restart the search, even if it results in a delay in hiring or causes frustrations on the part of committee members. The consequences of an inappropriate hire are too costly.

Communication

One of the most common concerns on college campuses is the belief that communication needs to be improved. Sometimes this occurs because of the way colleges operate in departments (or silos) with little interaction between them. College faculty, staff, and administrators are very busy people who sometimes don't take the time to communicate adequately—or to pay attention to what is communicated. The issues that are most sensitive, such as plans or decisions that affect the college's people, its mission, the strategies that are utilized to accomplish the mission, and the effectiveness of those strategies need to be the most publically communicated.

Brief summaries of meetings of governance committees should be posted in a timely manner on the college's intranet with links to the official agendas and minutes. Dashboards or a Gantt chart model should be devised to show the progress of college projects toward measurable goals. Members of governance committees should be reminded that they need to take responsibility to communicate regularly with their constituencies. College leaders can schedule periodic meetings on campuses at convenient times to discuss important college issues and to provide employees an opportunity to ask questions. Leaders can seek opportunities to bring employees together across the campus or campuses for more social interaction.

Collective Bargaining

Laws in several states grant public employees the right to join unions and to bargain collectively for wages, hours, and working conditions. Twenty-five states have passed "right to work" laws that restrict or prohibit collective bargaining. Some community college leaders prefer working in a nonunion environment because of the adversarial relationships that develop in a unionized college between "labor" and "management." Sometimes the hard feelings that are caused by difficult negotiations are lasting and interfere with the unity needed to accomplish institutional goals. However, the lack of employee unions does not guarantee there will be no hostility in negotiations between college and employee leaders. Paul Elsner, chancellor emeritus of the Maricopa Community College District in Arizona told George Boggs that discussions about wages, hours, and working conditions in a non-union district was like "killing without rules."

There are advantages to collective bargaining. It defines a process for coming to agreement, and it results in a contract that spells out the policies for both employees and college leaders to follow. Another advantage is that the contract is good for a specified number of years. Without a collective bargaining contract, negotiations can begin at any time; bargaining is never over.

The Los Rios and San Diego Community College Districts in California have developed systems to minimize the adversarial nature of collective bargaining. The districts have agreed on a predetermined formula that splits new revenue between employee groups and the college districts. The employee groups have discretion as to how they decide to use their portion of the new revenue. The agreements have "trombone clauses" that cause the contracts to be reopened in the event that revenues decline. However, neither district has had to utilize these provisions. Some leaders, however, may disagree with the approach used by the Los Rios and San Diego Community College Districts because a predetermined formula for salaries removes the monetary inducement for bargaining other contract provisions.

Collective bargaining should be separate from college governance, but it often overlaps. The faculty and staff leadership involved in college governance committees are the same people involved in union negotiations. The involvement of faculty and staff in governance has created some legal issues about the definitions of labor and management. In 2015, the National Labor Relations Board (NRLB) cleared the way for faculty at private universities to be represented by unions (Jaschik, 2015). Union representation was limited in1980 by the US Supreme Court decision in *NRLB v. Yeshiva University*, which determined that tenure-track faculty at private universities could not bargain collectively because they had managerial control. Although it was not successful, the Ohio legislature has considered limiting collective bargaining rights for public college and university faculty because of their managerial responsibilities (Farkas, 2015).

Whether participatory governance gives employees enough managerial control to be considered managers is debatable. But leaders must be careful not to agree to contract language that jeopardizes the future financial viability of the college or that creates obstacles for leaders to do their jobs. We have seen contract language that guarantees salary increases when future funding is uncertain and language that limits the ability of college administrators to schedule classes at times and locations needed by students.

Civility

Those who have chosen careers in community colleges are fortunate in many ways. College faculty, staff, trustees, and administrators make it possible for people to learn and to realize their dreams for a better future. For the most part, employees control a large percentage of their work schedules, work in attractive environments on college campuses or education centers, and work with intelligent and highly motivated colleagues. Some would call education a calling rather than a career or a profession because of the passion that many have to improve communities and the lives of students. Surveys consistently reveal a high level of public respect for community college educators and leaders.

Yet, despite these seeming advantages, stories abound of how poorly people treat each other in higher education institutions (Boggs, 2005). Those who have been involved in community college education for long enough will have witnessed poor treatment of students, disruptive behaviors on the part of students, mean-spirited behavior among colleagues in department or committee meetings, lack of respect for classified support staff, hostility between administrators and faculty, and dysfunctional boards of trustees that set a tone for incivility. At the very least, these behaviors detract from the very positive work with students and communities. In some cases, incivility on campus leads to health problems, threats of violence, and premature death. At the extreme, some college leaders have had to employ security guards for themselves and their families and even, in at least one case, to work behind a bulletproof shield.

How educators, leaders, and policy makers behave sets a tone for behavior of others even beyond campuses. Moreover, once a climate and patterns of behavior are set on a campus, they are difficult to change. New employees, students, and leaders enter an environment that has been created by those who came before. Nonetheless, college leaders have the power to affect the environment and to set a model for the kind of behavior that institutions, students, faculty and staff, and communities deserve.

Incivility can range from a thoughtless remark to purposefully intimi-dating, demeaning, hateful speech and to behaviors that can be mean-spirited and even threatening. In some cases, the campus environment may cause a student to drop out or an employee to become ill or to leave. Trustees, leaders, and faculty members have an opportunity to improve the learning and working environments on their campuses by making them more civil places.

Whenever highly intelligent, articulate, and caring people are brought together in one place, as they are on a college campus, one can expect that many different issues arise, and not everyone will agree on the best course of action. This environment is one that can yield a very healthy, studied, and respectful discussion of issues and courses of action so that the best decisions are made. At the same time, bad behavior on the part of a few individuals can convert this situation into one of distrust and hostility.

Debates about sensitive societal issues in communities often spill over onto college campuses, inviting behaviors that test the limits of civility. Examples range from antiwar demonstrations, to Israeli–Palestinian vio-lence, to police actions against unarmed African American males. Discussions of tuition cost increases often incite student activism. Reichman (2014) believes that efforts on the part of administrators to create a civil environment can infringe upon the right of freedom of speech. Campus leaders need to walk a fine line in stating their expecta-tions for civility and protecting the safety of students and employees while also protecting freedom of expression, even on the most controver-sial issues.

Anger caused by insufficient funding can be a cause of incivility; there are reports of an increasing number of votes of no confidence in the lead-ership of CEOs as they deal with cuts in state funding. College leaders are faced with few alternatives to difficult decisions that affect positions, benefits, and working conditions for employees and tuition costs and available course sections for students. Employees sometimes take their frustrations out on the college leadership.

A long-term community college leader told George Boggs that he believed that "friends may come and go, but enemies accumulate." With almost every decision a leader makes, there are people on the opposite side of the issue. Even if these people may be on the leader's side of an issue in the future, they always remember when they were not. Eventually, a critical mass of unhappy people might use uncivil behavior in an attempt to make it impossible for a leader to be effective. People who oppose a leader's decisions often look for ways to bring the leader down.

Academia seems to value egalitarianism, even to the extent of not wanting to see others recognized for excellence; but even more often, this value conflicts with the acceptance of authority. Although the governance systems of colleges are usually designed for inclusiveness and involvement of all, the colleges are not democracies, and someone in authority has to be responsible for decisions and their outcomes. The tension caused by superimposing the authority and responsibility of leadership on campuses that resist it can be a source of incivility.

Tenure laws were designed to protect the academic freedom of faculty members and to allow them to examine controversial subjects and sometimes to express unpopular points of view in their classrooms. Yet these protections often can be effective shields for bad behavior toward students, classified staff, and administrators.

Rude behavior is often not even noticed by those who exhibit it. Students who are continually late for class and employees who are perpetually late for meetings and appointments may not recognize this behavior as an act of incivility. The same might be said of those who allow cell phones to interrupt a class, a conference presentation, or a meeting. However, even those who engage in more serious acts of incivility may not recognize how disruptive they are. If they do, they usually feel their behavior is justified. Some people do not even recognize the degree of harm and pain caused by their behavior.

Some individuals may even derive a sense of reward from the divisiveness they engender and may thrive on the pain and even demise of others. As a college president, George Boggs talked with a very bright and articulate faculty member who had the potential to develop into an effective and positive campus leader. However, she was always very negative and seemed to be a disruptive influence. During a conversation, she revealed that the behavior was purposeful, and that she believed it was the source of her power. Because others saw that she was bold enough to exhibit negative behavior, they sought her help with their problems, and she felt valued by them. In the end, her negative behavior limited her career.

In a recent study, O'Banion (2015) found that every community college has a curmudgeon; most colleges have more than one. They are highly visible on campus and can be identified easily by faculty, staff, and administrators. Curmudgeons are contrarians who take enormous pleasure and pride in thinking otherwise. They can be cantankerous naysayers acting as self-appointed gadflies to the president or other leaders, including leaders of their own constituencies. Collaboration and civility do not seem to be values they hold in high esteem. They are quite vocal and opinionated and appear to prefer heated debate and prolonged circular discussion to solving problems and reaching consensus. Curmudgeons can be memorable characters with a certain flair or style, often using humor and sarcasm to play to their audiences.

Collective bargaining is a process that often uses incivility and bad behavior as a strategy. Unions can create an environment in which people feel free to behave uncivilly. Sometimes management teams also participate in these negative games of posturing. After the bargaining is concluded, people expect things to go back the way they were. Unfortunately, the hurt and damage caused by hostile negotiations may last for years and affect the climate of an institution.

Some administrators purposefully try to intimidate people in order to keep problems from emerging and becoming visible. Perhaps they are unsure of their leadership ability and believe that, if problems are unreported, they can deny their existence and not have to deal with them. In some cases, leaders single out opposition leaders for personal ridicule and defamation. Although this behavior on the part of a leader may be unusual, there may be leaders who, though not actively encouraging bad behavior, may not discourage it, either. Even after such a leader leaves a campus, the negative climate and level of distrust may linger.

Votes of no confidence are examples of strategic use of incivility. Faculty and staff may see them as their only weapons against a poor or intimidating leader. However, there are no consistent rules governing the purpose and use of these votes. The votes no longer signify a lack of integrity, competence, or ethical behavior. Instead, they are a strong protest against any leadership action with which people disagree. Often they are taken in response to stalled salary or contract negotiations rather than poor leadership. They seem to be more common in difficult financial times when leaders are faced with difficult decisions. It seems that sometimes employees need someone to blame for a bad situation, and the leader is a convenient person to blame. Administrative reorganizations are another frequent cause of votes of no confidence. Faculty members often strongly resist changes in how things are done.

Of course, leaders can and often do survive votes of no confidence. The vote that counts is that of the board of trustees or the system administrator. Moreover, votes of no confidence at one institution can affect job prospects at another. Frequently, mean-spirited individuals try to make sure they do. However, a wise search committee and board of trustees will do well to examine the circumstances of the vote.

Electronic communication and social media have made it possible for mean-spirited people to be even more effective in their uncivil behavior. They allow people to disseminate rude or damaging remarks throughout the campus and beyond. Some people have used these methods to send negative, often unsubstantiated, messages to campuses where someone is a candidate for a position.

Leaders must never react in kind to defend themselves and should resist the temptation to punish those who are attacking. The leader must set the tone for the behavior of others. However, leaders do have an obligation to confront instances of incivility against others. People can disagree, but they must be professional. No one, including students, staff, faculty, administrators, or trustees should be subjected to mean-spirited behavior, and the CEO is often in the best position to say what is unacceptable.

For a leader to survive attacks of incivility, it is important that he or she understand the dynamics of behavior on the part of groups such as the faculty and governing boards. These groups are more likely to provide support to the leader if the attacks are external. However, groups seem to be very reluctant to confront unacceptable behavior among their peers. Support from the community can strengthen both the external and internal positions of a leader, but the development of community support requires a long-term commitment. The media often plays an important role in times of crisis. It is important for leaders to respond appropriately to the interest of representatives of the media while respecting the legal necessity for some things to be confidential. Leaders always set the tone for their institutions, but this is never truer than when a leader is under attack.

It is important for institutions to develop codes of conduct that apply to all members of the campus community. Expectations for behavior should be communicated clearly to new faculty and staff members as well as to new members of the board of trustees. Leaders and board members must set the tone for behavior at the college in the same way that a faculty member must for the classroom. Leaders need to provide the support for faculty and staff members when they confront unacceptable behavior on the part of students. And leaders must not confuse civility with limitations on academic freedom and freedom of speech. In fact, civility and tolerance are necessary for the full realization of these freedoms.

Of course, codes of conduct do not always ensure good behavior. Although a code of conduct or code of ethics may not be all that is needed, it is clearly necessary to state what behavior is expected. The code must be visibly displayed, and people need to be periodically reminded about the expectations that it sets. The topic of civility should be included as a part of orientation of new employees and new board members.

It is all too common on college campuses to see a lack of respect for classified or support staff. They are often not treated with the same deference that is shown to faculty and academic administrators. Yet they are essential to the operation of our colleges. They are often the very first people contacted by students, prospective students, and community members. Leaders must be sure to communicate the importance of these employees to the mission of the institution, and the codes of conduct must apply to how support staff members are treated. A class system for behavior toward employees has no place in the colleges of democracy.

Issues to Consider

A. What strategies might be effective in dealing with a rogue trustee?

B. What problems might be created by having trustee offices on a college campus or at the district office?

C. As a college president, George Boggs received a telephone call from a trustee who was a medical doctor. The trustee told the president to fire an adjunct emergency medical technician instructor because, even though she was a registered nurse, she was not teaching properly. The president found that no evaluation of the adjunct instructor had been done and directed the vice president for instruction to evaluate the instructor. The vice president's evaluation report showed that the instructor was doing a good job and was popular with the hospital staff, but that she had been in an argument with the medical doctor who was the college trustee. When the president reported to the trustee that the evaluation was positive and the instructor should be allowed to continue, the trustee insisted that the president fire the instructor. What issues are involved in this case? How would you respond?

D. In a unionized environment, what can be done to keep collective bargaining and participatory governance issues separate?

E. In his 2012 article in the *Chronicle of Higher Education,* Rob Jenkins discussed three strategies for college leaders to deal with faculty dissent. The first is to punish or make examples of the disagreeable people; the second is to ignore and isolate the dissenters; and the third is to treat the dissenters, as much as possible, like anyone else. Which strategy is usually the best in dealing with negativity? Are there times when each of the strategies might be effective?

F. In October 2014, shortly after Walla Walla Community College shared the Aspen Prize for being one of the best community colleges in the nation, a local newspaper in Washington State reported that the faculty voted no confidence in its president (http://m.union-bulletin.com/news/2014/oct/18/faculty-votes-no-confidence-wwcc-president/). What were the apparent causes of the vote? What actions should a president take after a vote of no confidence?

G. Shortly after the massacre of the children at Sandy Hook Elementary School in Newtown, Connecticut, in 2012, Scott Jaschik reported in *Inside Higher Ed* that a professor at Florida Atlantic University had been blogging about his doubts that the massacre really took place, speculating that the Obama administration had made up the story to advance a gun-control agenda. The university later fired the professor after receiving a letter of complaint from the parents who lost a son at Sandy Hook. The university did not give a reason for firing the tenured professor. Is the speculation of the professor protected by academic freedom? If the termination of employment was related to the professor's denial of the massacre, is the action justified?

H. Tenure has recently come under attack, with the most visible debate arising from the case *Vergara v. California*, in which the judge struck down tenure in public schools as illegally discriminating against children who attended schools in the most economically challenged areas. (See http://www.huffingtonpost.com/2014/08/12/teachers-unions-yougov-poll_n_5669090.html.) The decision does not affect higher education at this point, and the state is appealing. Will higher education tenure laws come under similar scrutiny at some point? What does tenure really mean? Does tenure inappropriately protect incompetent faculty? Are there ways to ensure that tenure protects academic freedom and not incompetence?

I. What risks are inherent in not having an up-to-date college media relations strategy? What are the risks of not having a social media governance plan? How can a college leadership team use social media to advance the mission of the college?

Case Scenario

You receive a memorandum from your college's faculty union president informing you that she is directing faculty not to comply with your request to address the recommendations from the previous college accreditation report because labor negotiations have been stalled. The accrediting commission has given college leadership six months to submit a report that details how the college is complying with the recommendations. What issues does the scenario create? What leadership competencies are involved? Who should be involved in addressing the situation? What actions would you take? Are there lessons to be learned?

REFERENCES

Ansaldo, M. (2015). Five Components of a Social Media Governance Model. *PC World*. Retrieved from: http://www.pcworld.com/article/250043/ 4_components_of_a_social_media_governance_model.html. Retrieved from: http://chronicle.com/article/Toward-a-Shared-Vision-of/151041.

Boggs, G. (2005). Civility on Campus. In P. Elsner & G. Boggs (Eds.), *Encouraging Civility as a Community College Leader* (pp. 1–12). Washington, DC: Community College Press.

Boggs, G. (2006). *Handbook on CEO-Board Responsibilities and Relationships*. Washington, DC: Community College Press.

Bowen, W. & Tobin, E. (2015, January 5). Toward a Shared Vision of Shared Governance. *Chronicle of Higher Education*. Retrieved from http:// chronicle.com/article/Toward-a-Shared-Vision-of/151041.

Carroll, C. E. (2004). How the Mass Media Influence Perceptions of Corporate Reputation: Exploring Agenda-Setting Effects Within Business News Coverage. Diss., University of Texas, Austin.

Cohen, J. R. (1999). Advising Clients to Apologize. *Southern California Law Review, 72*, 1009–1131.

Coombs, W. T. (1998). An Analytic Framework for Crisis Situations: Better Responses from a Better Understanding of the Situation. *Journal of Public Relations Research, 10*, 177–191.

Coombs, W. T., & Holladay, S. J. (2004). Reasoned Action in Crisis Communication: An Attribution Theory-Based Approach to Crisis Management. In D. P. Millar & R. L. Heath (Eds.), *Responding to Crisis: A Rhetorical Approach to Crisis Communication* (pp. 95–115). Mahwah, NJ: Erlbaum.

Dean, D. H. (2004). Consumer Reaction to Negative Publicity: Effects of Corporate Reputation, Response, and Responsibility for a Crisis Event. *Journal of Business Communication, 41*, 192–211.

Farkas, K. (2015). College Faculty Oppose Provision in New Budget Bill That Would Limit Collective Bargaining. *Cleveland.com*. Retrieved from: http:// www.cleveland.com/metro/index.ssf/2015/04/college_faculty_oppose_anti- un.html.

Fisher, J. L., & Koch, J. V. (1996). *Presidential Leadership: Making A Difference.* American Council on Education. Series on Higher Education. Phoenix, AZ: Oryx Press.

Ganim Barnes, N., & Lescault, A. (2011). *Social Media Adoption Soars as Higher-Ed Experiments and Reevaluates Its Use of New Communication Tools.* Dartmouth: University of Massachusetts Center for Marketing Research.

Jaschik, S. (2015). Big Union Win. *Inside Higher Ed.* Retrieved from: https://www.insidehighered.com/news/2015/01/02/nlrb-ruling-shifts-legal-ground-faculty-unions-private-colleges.

Jenkins, R. (2012). Dealing with Dissent. *Chronicle of Higher Education.* Retrieved from: http://chronicle.com/blogs/onhiring/dealing-with-dissent/31859.

O'Banion, T. (2009). *The Rogue Trustee: The Elephant in the Room.* Chandler, AZ: League for Innovation in the Community College.

O'Banion, T. (2015). *Community College Curmudgeons: Barriers to Change.* Chandler, AZ: League for Innovation in the Community College.

Parker, K., Lenhart, A., & Moor, K. (2011, August 28). *The Digital Revolution and Higher Education: College Presidents, Public Differ on Value of Online Learning.* Retrieved from: http://www.pewsocialtrends.org/2011/08/28/overview/.

Reichman, H. (2014). Civility and Free Speech. *Inside Higher Education.* Retrieved from: https://www.insidehighered.com/views/2014/10/14/essay-argues-recent-statements-college-leaders-about-civility-are-threat-academic.

Solis, B. (2008). *Introducing the Conversation Prism.* Retrieved from: http://www.briansolis.com/ 2008/08/introducing-conversation-prism.html.

Zaiontz, D., & Stoner, M. (Ed.) (2015). *#Follow the Leader: Lessons in Social Media from #HigherED CEOs.* St. Louis, Missouri: EDUuniverse Media.

7

ORGANIZATIONAL CHANGE TO PROMOTE STUDENT SUCCESS

Leading Organizational Change

Community colleges have a proud history of serving their communities, but they are in the midst of an evolution that will more clearly focus increasingly limited resources on the success of their students. Like many institutions that have several years of history, the policies, practices, and structures that may have worked in an earlier time no longer make sense in an era of constrained resources, increased accountability for student success, and the demand to close achievement gaps. Leaders frequently encounter practices that are historically based and perhaps memorialized in college policies or union contracts that prove to be hindrances to effective management of the colleges and their ability to serve students and their communities.

Leaders are often selected for their positions with a mandate to implement changes in their institutions. Both new and existing leaders might be asked to deal with institutional problems that include financial or accounting issues, low employee morale, enrollment decline, poor community relations, or a need to improve student success rates. However, changing higher educational institutions is rarely an easy task, and it can be risky. Leaders invariably encounter resistance and, sometimes, hostility, and they may even lose support for needed changes and perhaps even their jobs if changes are not approached carefully. It is wise to approach change cautiously and gradually. Leaders should not try to initiate too much change at once. When George Boggs was a new college president, a seasoned leader cautioned him to "pick your battles." There are always a great many practices, procedures, and policies that need to be revised, but a wise leader should focus on the most important ones and those that are possible to change first.

Daniel Phelan, President of Jackson College in Michigan, points out how important it is for a college president to have the full support of the board of trustees before initiating significant institutional change. He relates a particularly meaningful interaction he had at a retreat with the seven-member board of trustees at Jackson College about driving institutional change through the collective bargaining contract negotiations process. He said to the board members, "If I am going to deal with this issue, I want to know that when things get rough—and they will—that when I am pushed back one step, I will feel fourteen hands on my back." The board members all agreed and lived up to that commitment (Phelan, 2016, p. 84). Although top-down directives can work in private businesses, they do not often succeed in public higher education. A more appropriate approach for higher education might be to follow the example of the leaders who facilitated social change, leaders such as Martin Luther King, Jr., who, standing in the shadows of the symbols of our nation, pointed out that our country was not living up to its own democratic ideals while he described a vision of a better future for all of our people.

People are often less resistant to change when there is a clear need, especially during times of significant challenge to the institution. When Rahm Emanuel was chief of staff in the White House, he was famously quoted as saying, "You never want a serious crisis to go to waste." It is often much easier to implement organizational change during a recognized crisis. Recommendations from outside groups, especially accrediting agencies or consultants who are recognized authorities, can also help leaders bring about change. Affiliation with nationally recognized projects, such as Achieving the Dream or Completion by Design that intend to bring about improvement in outcomes, can be effective in getting the necessary internal support for change. The models described in this chapter can be utilized for any desired organizational change. For illustration, one of today's most urgent challenges—improving student success rates—is the change described in this chapter.

Policy makers, researchers, and educators are in the midst of an extended national debate about the very future of community colleges. The narrative not only challenges programs and services offered by the community college sector but also the policies and practices that implement them. The demand to improve college completion rates is at the center of the current call for change, one that both critics and advocates label the "Completion Agenda" (American Association of Community Colleges [AACC], 2010; Complete College America, 2014; MDRC, 2013). The core concern is that students are not completing what they start, and community colleges can and must do better. To advance the Completion Agenda, institutions must change.

The Completion Agenda

The focus of the debate about student success is on organizational change, the need for it, and whether community colleges are up to the challenges. Although access to higher education is still an issue for some populations, the concern most commonly expressed today is that not enough students are progressing through the institution and attaining degrees or certificates or transferring to four-year colleges and universities. Traditionally, community colleges have stressed access, especially for underrepresented students. Community colleges enroll large numbers of low-income, adult, and minority students, providing educational opportunities that were not available to these students at other institutions. The access to education and training and the opportunities provided by community colleges are the reasons they are referred to as the "open-door" colleges. As important as access and opportunity are, however, they are not sufficient. As early as 2000, Robert McCabe, president emeritus of Miami Dade College, argued that it was necessary to guarantee quality in order to keep the "open door" open. McCabe observed that, even though hundreds of underprepared college students enter community colleges, many of these students successfully complete remediation and go on to do as well in standard college courses as those students who begin academically prepared (Callan, 2000; McCabe, 2000). Leaders of the community college movement are often asked, "How can community colleges respond to the Completion Agenda without sacrificing either the open-door mission or academic rigor?" As educational reform and accountability efforts—especially since 2010—have placed an increasing number of demands on community colleges nationwide, the leaders of local institutions have been forced to reevaluate their commitment to both access and student success. There are a number of ways community colleges can improve student success rates while maintaining or even improving access and quality, and all of them require a commitment to organizational change and to thinking differently about how to use resources to educate, train, and support students (Alfred & Carter, 1999; AACC, 2013).

As a first step, community college leaders must acknowledge that existing policies, practices, programs, and services are not producing the desired results. It is important to set appropriate goals for improvement before developing corresponding change strategies to achieve them. Leaders need to identify the key stakeholders and their roles in realizing the vision of the future of the institution (AACC, 2012). Finally, in implementing change, community college leaders will need to more effectively utilize resources and the skill sets of employees to produce desired results. In short, organizational change must go beyond changes in strategic planning models or changes in job descriptions, as important as they are. Effective organizational change must involve all constituent groups: boards of trustees, administrators, faculty, staff, students, and community partners (AACC, 2012; Kotter, 2008). Essentially, colleges will have to make necessary adjustments in the way they conduct the business of the institution in order to produce the desired results (AACC, 2012).

Leaders need to create an environment in which the college community can work collaboratively to define the changes needed and to develop strategies to respond to the diverse learning needs of students. Active leadership support to incorporate a variety of innovative strategies and new policies and procedures is necessary to improve student pathways to learning that stimulate, bring to scale, and institutionalize an effective array of learning experiences (Jacobs & Dougherty, 2006; Watson, Williams, & Derby, 2005).

Models for Change

There are many ways of thinking about organizational change that can apply to community colleges (Kotter, 2008; Maginn, 2005; Weick, 1995). As colleges struggle with the challenges of the Completion Agenda, leaders need to undertake a careful review of the role and purpose of the institution (AACC, 2012). At the same time, leaders must define the process by which the college should determine changes in structure, strategies, operational methods, technologies, or organizational culture and assess the effects of those changes on the organization (AACC, 2014; Floyd, Haley, Eddy, & Antczak, 2009). Leaders must always be aware of the fact that organizational change can be contentious, time-consuming, highly political, and, at times, risky to the career of a leader.

Van de Ven and Poole (1995) argued that change is measured by the observation of difference over time in one or more dimensions of an institution. Burnes (1996) noted that organizational change requires understanding alterations within organizations at the broadest level among individuals and groups and at the collective level across the entire organization. However, these general descriptions of change do not entirely capture factors inherent in community colleges such as the demographics of stakeholders and their values. It can be informative to think of change through a cultural or social-cognition lens, focusing on values and beliefs of the stakeholders within the organization. Although there is no single model for organizational change, certain concepts are common across change models, such as the overlap between elements of the Kotter (2008) and Lewin (2007) models. For example, Kurt Lewin's model proposed a straightforward change management process consisting of a three-stage theory of change commonly referred to as unfreeze, change, freeze (or refreeze). Kotter (2008) believed that change followed a process consisting of eight sequential phases:

1. A sense of urgency
2. The guiding team
3. Visions and strategies
4. Communication
5. Empowerment
6. Celebrating short-term wins
7. Never letting up
8. Making change stick

Both models examine why change happens and refer to outcomes of the change process. Based in observational theory, these models can assist leaders as they prepare to chart a course for change in their colleges. In particular, when colleges engage in a change process, constituent groups need to know why change is important, how much change is needed, and what might be the best approach to implement the change (Gumport, 2000).

Resistance to Change

Community college leaders who want to improve their institutions must carefully determine the changes that will move their institutions toward desired goals (AACC, 2012). The changes that community colleges will need to make should align with the core values of the institution (Alfred et al., 2009; Erwin, 1997; Kim & Mauborgne, 2003). However, institutional leadership is embedded in a network of influence and power that comes from a variety of sources. Leaders cannot assume that all of the sources will even agree that change is necessary. Even if they do, they may not agree on what needs to be changed or what strategies to use. Leadership within this context calls for an effective analysis of stakeholder values and resistance to change. What does resistance to change look like? What are its causes, and where does it come from? Resistance to change can emerge from both internal and external sources and can be viewed as the act of opposing or struggling with modifications or transformations that alter the status quo in the workplace (Kotter, 1998).

Overcoming resistance to change is often extremely challenging. Although Burke (2008) argued that organizations strive to succeed in an increasingly complex global, political, and economic environment that requires change to remain viable, he noted that organizations experience different types of change, and some changes are more difficult than others. Resistance to change can emerge from internal or external groups or individuals. It can be covert or overt, organized or spontaneous. In some instances, resistance emerges when there is a threat to something the individual values. For example, Evans (2001), in discussing the human side of school change, noted that resistance may arise either from a genuine understanding of the change or from a misunderstanding of the issues. Failure to adequately consider the complexity of the resistance can compromise the implementation of the change or even stop it. Viable change requires the involvement of the entire campus community. Resistance to change can affect the entire institution in areas such as the feelings, opinions, and work habits of employees at all stages of implementation of the change process.

If community college leaders are to be successful in implementing change, they must first examine the key reasons people might resist it. Implementing change involves altering human behavior and the acceptance of change. According to John Tagg (2012), one of the leading spokespersons for the Learning Paradigm:

> The key to designing and executing productive institutional change is not simply to build a better academic mousetrap. Faculty will not beat a path to the doors of those with the best arguments. We need to not only design change for our institutions but also redesign our institutions for change. At base, we must recognize that we can't change without changing. We cannot create a better future unless we are willing to embrace a future that is different from the past. (p. 6)

There are a number of reasons people resist change: a lack of clarity of the rationale for the change, a lack of appropriate consultation and communication, a perceived threat caused by the change, or weak perceived benefits and rewards for making the change (Demers, 2007; Erwin, 2009; Kotter 2008).

Resistance Management

Strebel (2006) observed that the reason for the less than favorable success rate in leading change is differences between the perceptions of leadership and employees. It is necessary to develop a distinctive approach that bridges these perceptions in order to change higher education (Hearn, 1996). Hearn noted that overlooking these factors may result in mistakes in analysis and strategy, and using concepts foreign to the values of the academy will most likely fail to engage the very people who must bring about the change.

The leader must be able to identify and manage resistance at different levels of the organization (Benjamin & Carroll, 1996; Maginn, 2005). In an organization that has a culture of trust, transparent communication, involvement, engaged employees, and positive interpersonal relationships, resistance to change is easy to see—and also much less likely to occur (Kotter, 2008). In this type of environment, employees feel free to tell the leadership team what they think and to have open exchanges with unit administrators. When a change is introduced in institutions in which people feel engaged, the resistance to change is decreased. Resistance is also minimized if there is a widespread belief that a change is needed. The president and leadership team must communicate the need for change and must highlight the consequences that may develop if the change is delayed. Kotter (1995) recommended that effective communication should be used to promote or market the proposed changes, while at the same time demonstrating the shortcomings of the old way of doing business.

One of the key factors in reducing resistance to change is widespread acceptance that a change is needed. So, one of the first tasks for the leader is to build the case for the reasons for change (Amey, VanDerLinden, & Brown, 2002). Specifically, the leader must first inform the college community about the need for change. But it does not stop with an information session. The leader must engage the campus community in active dialogue and spend time discussing the urgency for change, how to implement the change, and how to make it work. Among the major reasons for engaging the campus community in conversations about change is that leaders can share their vision for a better future and personally identify the benefits of change to individuals, departments, and the organization. Further, stakeholders must feel that the time, energy, commitment, and focus necessary to implement the change are compensated by the benefits they, the institution, and students will attain from making the change.

Employee Pride as Motivation for Change

Most community college educators and staff members are proud of their colleges and the work they do, but these are challenging times for community colleges as pressure builds to improve the ways they meet the needs of the students and communities they serve. Leaders interested in facilitating organizational change must understand the critical link between the employee's pride in the institution and willingness to support organizational changes. Jon Katzenbach (2003) recommended that senior management sponsor and support activities to inspire employees to take pride in the organization. Katzenback made the point that "pride is more powerful than money. Employee pride—the admiration of co-workers as well as family and friends, the spirit of teams in pursuit of a dream, and the high that comes from having done a job well—is the powerful motivational force that compels individuals and companies to excel" (p. 24).

Community college leaders can build upon employees' pride in the organization by ensuring that the mission, vision, and institutional goals are made clear to all employees and to let them know how their work supports the college mission. Leaders must strive to help all employees take pride in their work and to understand how their work contributes to institutional excellence. Helping employees to take pride in their jobs takes time and effort. Individual pride in the organization and the buy-in to overall instructional excellence cannot be mandated. Leaders must make pride-building a continuing part of their leadership agenda.

We have visited a great many community college campuses and are often told by faculty and administrators, "Our college is the best community college in the country." It is always rewarding to hear the sense of pride that employees have, but we often wonder what data the colleges have to back up the claims. Leaders should recognize and celebrate the pride that employees have in their college and then use outcome data to show that the college can help more students to succeed. Then, leaders should ask for recommendations from the employees about how to improve.

Organizational Change and Classroom Practice

Community colleges have made some meaningful changes in the teaching and learning environment to help more students experience success (Achieving the Dream, 2012). The following teaching and learning practices illustrate some of the most promising strategies that have been shown to be beneficial for community college students from a variety of backgrounds. These practices can take many different forms, depending on learner characteristics and on institutional priorities and contexts.

1. Guided Pathways

As mentioned in chapter 2, in October 2015, AACC announced a national partnership to build capacity for community colleges to implement a pathways approach to student success and college completion (Bailey, Jaggers, & Jenkins, 2015). There is almost universal agreement that giving entering students more guidance is necessary if we are to improve rates of student success. Davis Jenkins, senior researcher at the Community College Research Center (CCRC) at Columbia University and an early proponent of guided pathways for students, has identified key components of the Guided Pathway model:

○ Clear road maps to success are provided and academic programs are clearly defined.

○ Exploratory majors are designed for students who do not have majors when they enter the college.

○ Contextualized instruction in foundation skills are linked to the student's field of interest.

○ Predictable schedules provide a defined program of study on a full-time and part-time basis.

○ Students are provided frequent feedback on how they are doing.

○ Colleges use early alert systems to keep students informed about their progress so that they can stay on track.

2. Flipped Classrooms

The flipped classroom is a pedagogical model in which the typical lecture and homework elements of a course are reversed. Students view short video lectures at home and read supporting text before the class session, and in-class time is devoted to exercises, projects, debates, or discussions. The video lecture is often seen as the key ingredient to the flipped approach; the instructor or guest presenters create the lectures that are posted online or selected from an online repository. The notion of a flipped classroom draws on such concepts as active learning, student engagement, hybrid course design, and course podcasting. The value of a flipped class is in the repurposing of in-class time into an active workshop in which students can inquire about course content, test their skills in applying knowledge, and interact with one another in hands-on activities. During class sessions, instructors act as facilitators, moderators, coaches, or advisors, encouraging students in individual inquiry and collaborative effort (Bichsel, 2012).

3. Online Classes

The convenience of online education has attracted working adult students who benefit from education delivered in ways that meet their schedules and the demands of working, family obligations, and social lives. However, learning under these circumstances is not easy. Major problems reported by students are feelings of isolation, lack of self-direction, time management, and eventual decrease in motivation (Ludwig-Hardman & Dunlap, 2003). Faculty who teach online courses must find ways to engage students, to keep them motivated, and to encourage them not to fall behind in their assignments.

4. Blended Classes/Learning

The traditional learning environment, especially lectures in which students are passive, simply does not engage most students. "Blended classes" utilize both the classroom environment and technology to meet the learning and motivational needs of students. Ideally, a blended classroom offers deeper content online, gives students the ability to master basic skills, and grants them more autonomy (Bonk & Graham, 2006).

5. Project-Based Learning

Project-based learning, focused on learning through engagement in individual or group assignments, is a meaning-oriented and student-centered instructional approach that allows students to discover content, engage in higher-level thinking, make personal connections, construct their own meaning, and reflect on what they have learned (Savage, 2007).

6. First-Year Seminars and Experiences

Many schools now build into the curriculum first-year seminars or other programs that bring small groups of students together with faculty or staff on a regular basis. First-year experiences place a strong emphasis on critical inquiry, frequent writing, information literacy, collaborative learning, and other skills that develop students' intellectual and practical competencies (Franklin, 2000; Gardner & Barefoot, 2011).

7. Learning Communities

The key goals for learning communities are to encourage integration of learning across courses and to involve students with "big questions" that matter beyond the classroom. Students take two or more linked courses as a group and work closely with one another and with their professors. Many learning communities explore a common topic and/or common readings through the lenses of different disciplines (Levine & Shapiro, 2004).

8. Collaborative Assignments and Projects

Collaborative learning combines two key goals: learning to work and solve problems in the company of others; and sharpening one's own understanding by listening seriously to the insights of others, especially those with different backgrounds and life experiences. Approaches range from study groups within a course, to team-based assignments and writing, to cooperative projects and research (Gabriel, 2004).

9. Service Learning and Community-Based Learning

Field-based "experiential learning" with community partners is an instructional strategy—and can be a required part of a course. The idea is to give students direct experience with issues they are studying in the curriculum and with ongoing efforts to analyze and solve problems in the community. A key element in these programs is the opportunity students have both to apply what they are learning in real-world settings and to reflect in a classroom setting on their service experiences (Hatcher, Bringle, & Muthiah, 2004).

10. Cooperative Work Experience

Internships, cooperative work experience, and apprenticeships are included in a wide range of integrated work and education strategies. Typically, institutions use an external worksite as a source to provide the skills training required for the program of study. Participating students earn college credit for their work experience attaining the skills and knowledge related to the program of study. Institutions use the cooperative work experience programs to bridge the gap between the institution and business and industry. Collaborative work experience programs also contribute to local economic development efforts by providing a flow of qualified and skilled employees for local business and industry partners (Cates & Cedercreutz, 2008).

11. Supplemental Instruction

Academic assistance programs that utilize peer-assisted study sessions are classified as supplemental instruction (SI). SI sessions are regularly scheduled, informal review sessions in which students compare notes, discuss readings, develop organizational tools, and work on predicted test items. Students learn how to integrate course content and study skills while working together. The sessions are facilitated by "SI leaders," students who have previously done well in the course and who attend all class lectures, take notes, and act as model students (Stone & Jacobs, 2008).

Organizational Change and Student Support Services

Simpson (2002) defined student support in the broadest terms as all activities beyond the production and delivery of course materials that assist in the progress of students in their studies. Support systems include tutorials, technical support, library resources and information services, advising or counseling, and peer support. According to Simpson (2002), there is clearly little point in providing a student service without connecting it to a demonstrated student need. In an attempt to better serve the contemporary student, community colleges have made changes in the types of support services offered. The following list highlights some of the key enhancements to student support programs offered to provide services aligned with the mission of the college.

1. Electronic Tutorial Support

Since distance education students often report a feeling of isolation, it is crucial to have online problem and discussion sessions, known as tutorials. According to Vincent and Eisenstadt (1998), the benefit of tutorials is only partly academic; the tutorial is an important social support system that allows students to build relationships with their instructors and other students (Garrison & Anderston, 2003).

2. Virtual Office Hours

Within an online course, instructors may be perceived as inaccessible when they do not respond in a timely fashion (Howland & Moore, 2002). One solution is to schedule online virtual hours (e-office hours) (preferably after 6:00 p.m.) and days for students to contact the instructor via email, telephone, and/or chat rooms.

3. Help Desks and Technical Support

The most common practice is to have an online help desk available to students at all times, during which support personnel can reply through email or chat to assist with issues like password and access problems.

4. Online Counseling (or Personal Tutor)

Counseling services, like tutoring and technical support, can be scheduled to give advice and information to students on a wide range of educational, financial, and practical issues (Mallen, Vogel, Rochlen, & Day, 2005).

5. Online One-Stop Centers

"One-stop" is a student services model that relies heavily on highly developed and intuitive online portals, sophisticated transaction-enabling self-service, cross-trained staff, and thorough integration of "traditional" services such as registration, financial aid, and billing all under one roof (or two roofs really: one digital and one physical). This model is student-centered and technologically rich, and, from a student's perspective, simple. It aims also to liberate institutions from archaic, inefficient, often redundant models suited for a bygone era (Burnett & Oblinger, 2002).

6. Learning Analytics

Learning analytics emerged from the business sector and are designed to help institutions learn more about student trends and, to some extent, predict behavior patterns of students. Learning analytics enhance the institution's capacity to build large data bases that can be used to improve teaching and learning effectiveness. For example, learning analytics are the foundation for early alert programs that signal when a student is struggling, allowing instructors and advisors to intervene in time to assist students before they fail (Gonzalez, 2012).

7. Gaming

The games culture has grown to include a substantial proportion of the world's population, with the age of the average gamer increasing with each passing year. Community college educators have discovered 'that games can be used to teach cross-curricular concepts that touch on many subjects in a more engaging way than traditional teaching methods.

For example, Cuyahoga Community College implemented a project called Edugaming Positively that has improved college completion rates. The college also established the Gaming Incubation Group that creates games and encourages their use in both face-to-face and online learning: go.nmc.org/games (Wu, 2012).

8. Social Media

Many community college educators are attracted to social media because it enables institutions to employ two-way communication between existing and prospective students. Using such tools as Facebook and Twitter, instructors can establish and maintain interactions with students that were not possible in traditional teaching and learning environments. For example, educators can use video platforms such as YouTube and Vimeo to reach students and share lectures and other classrooms activities that students can access from anywhere and at any time (Gesser, 2013).

A Time for Change: AACC's Reclaiming the American Dream

Community college leaders have two choices: they can change the students they serve or they can change their support services and teaching and learning approaches to accommodate the students they have. In the first instance, community colleges can require that students who enroll must possess demonstrated college-level skill sets. This approach would likely increase college completion rates, but it would also result in diminished access to higher education for a high percentage of low-income and minority students. In the second scenario, community colleges are confronted with the challenge of making changes in the manner in which they accommodate the diverse learning and support needs of their students (DeMers, 2007).

The reform initiatives, including those advocated by AACC, call for community colleges leaders to understand the change process. Calls for change are not new for higher education. In 1996, Barrow encouraged higher education institutions to look at strategies for selective excellence that could better position American higher education institutions for global competiveness. The recent reform initiatives that are focused on changing community colleges to promote higher levels of student success are, in many ways, a continuation of work to address long-term challenges. Bailey and colleagues (2015) make a persuasive argument for the type of changes that are needed to help more community college students succeed.

In AACC's 2012 *Reclaiming the American Dream*, Walter G. Bumphus, President and CEO of the American Association of Community Colleges, challenges community colleges to "redesign, reinvent, and reset (The 3 Rs). We need to completely reimagine community colleges for today and the future" (AACC, 2012, p. VI).

The 3 Rs consist of the following: *redesign* students' educational experiences, *reinvent* institutional roles, and *reset* the system to create incentives for student and institutional success. The specific recommendations of the 3 Rs can serve as both motivation and guidance for a change agenda for community colleges.

1. **Increase completion rates** of students earning community college credentials (certificates and associate's degrees) by 50 percent by 2020, while preserving access, enhancing quality, and eradicating attainment gaps associated with income, race, ethnicity, and gender.

2. **Dramatically improve college readiness.** By 2020, reduce by half the number of students entering college unprepared for rigorous college-level work and double the number of students who complete developmental education programs and progress to successful completion of related freshman-level courses.

3. **Close the American skills gaps** by sharply focusing career and technical education on preparing students with the knowledge and skills required for existing and future jobs in regional and global economies.

4. **Refocus the community college mission** and redefine institutional roles to meet twenty-first-century education and employment needs.

5. **Invest in support structures** to serve multiple community colleges through collaboration among institutions and with partners in philanthropy, government, and the private sector.

6. **Strategically target public and private investments** to create new incentives for institutions to educate and train their students and to support community college efforts to reclaim the American Dream.

7. **Implement policies and practices** that promote rigor, transparency, and accountability for results in community colleges.

If implementing the organizational changes recommended by AACC's *Reclaiming the American Dream* report is considered a prescription for changing the community college, what actions can leaders take to realize the expected outcomes? Only time will tell if community colleges have the capacity to meet the challenges, but community colleges have evolved throughout their history to respond to the needs of society. Today's challenges will require them to shift some basic assumptions and long-held traditions about the support they should provide to students and the need to raise expectations for student performance. Some community college educators will need to open their minds to serve learners through a different array of programs and delivery systems. It will not be enough for community colleges to continue making changes through collections of scattered pilot interventions (MDRC, 2013). Far too often, reform efforts have focused on starting pilot program after pilot program. While the pilots unleash a lot of small and often positive interventions, they are usually isolated and do not lead to sustained or scalable outcomes. Community colleges must find ways to stimulate and bring to scale changes across the institutions—as well as to sustain those changes—if they are to create models that can serve the expanding needs of twenty-first-century learners.

Sustaining Momentum: Managing the Change

Often, the most difficult period in managing change is the final phase, when leaders work to adjust plans and sustain the momentum of implementation. Change efforts often encounter a wide variety of obstacles—for example, strong resistance from members of the organization, untimely departure of a key leader in the organization, or a dramatic and sudden reduction in finances (Aune, 1995).

Stober (2008) suggested that coaching could be used as a tool to sustain change. He points out that coaching can guide employees through the change process. Leaders are encouraged to provide clear messages to achieve organizational acceptance of the process. Internal and external environmental pressures that influence institutional effectiveness; organizational inefficiency; and student, faculty, and staff dissatisfaction are additional issues that can impede the change process (Burke, 2011). In fact, most change initiatives do not succeed and last (Senge et al., 2008). Strong, visible, ongoing support from top leadership is critically important to show overall credibility and accountability in the change effort. How the leader communicates the change process to the stakeholders has an important impact on how much resistance there will be to the changes (Kotter, 2008). Everyone in an organization has a role to play in a performance transformation of the magnitude envisioned by the Completion Agenda. The role of CEOs is unique in that they stand at the top of the pyramid, and all the other members of the organization take cues from them. It is up to the leader to ensure that the right people spend the right amount of time driving the necessary changes.

Community college leaders can use technology as a vehicle for responding to societal changes (Waters, 2014). The *NMC Horizon Report: 2015 Higher Education Edition*, in partnership with the EDUCAUSE Learning Initiative (ELI), stated that improving digital literacy is considered one of the solvable challenges facing higher education. The report also identified two long-term objectives: (1) advancing learning environments that are flexible and drive innovation and (2) increasing the collaboration that takes place between higher education institutions. Organizational changes and enhanced technological developments can support innovation and improved outcomes in community colleges. The ELI report can serve as a planning guide for technology for community college educators (Waters, 2014). Those participating in change efforts often need training and coaching on how to implement change. The role of targeted professional development cannot be overstated when launching a change agenda.

It is important for leaders to use a change model or process that people can understand and follow. Kotter's (1997) change model, employing an eight-step process, is a good one to consider. His eight-phase model is summarized as follows:

1. **Establish a Sense of Urgency.** President Barack Obama's college completion challenge, the five national associations' call to action, the visibility of recent reform initiatives, and AACC's *Reclaiming the American Dream* all outline a sense of urgency for community colleges and can be used by leaders to launch a change effort to better serve students.

2. **Form a Powerful Guiding Coalition.** Kotter suggests that, during Phase 2, it is important to identify three to five people to lead the change effort. Involving respected leaders from key areas of the institution is critical to success of the change effort. Some leaders have found that an existing committee, such as a curriculum committee or a task force, can serve as a guiding coalition to launch a particular change effort.

3. **Create a Vision.** According to Kotter, "Vision helps clarify the direction in which an organization must pass in order to arrive at the desired future." One or more of AACC's 3 Rs can serve as an excellent platform to advance a vision and a meaningful agenda to improve student success.

4. **Communicate That Vision.** Kotter suggests that communicating the vision is needed and ongoing. It is not a single event. The principle is simple: use existing communication channels and identify opportunities to speak to the campus community on a regular basis about the change effort and its progress.

5. **Remove Obstacles.** Continually check for barriers to the change effort. The president and the leadership team can identify or hire change leaders whose main roles are to implement the change, identify people who are resisting the change, and help them see what's needed.

6. **Create Short-Term Wins.** Nothing motivates people more than success. Thoroughly analyze the progress toward meeting the change goals. If the process doesn't succeed with an early goal, it can hurt the entire change initiative. The people who help the institution meet the change targets can be rewarded on a routine and consistent basis.

7. **Build on the Change.** Kotter argues that many change projects fail because victory is declared too early. Real change runs deep. After every win, analyze what went right and what needs improving. The engagement of institutional research professionals can be useful by providing data and reports to support data-informed decision making to facilitate needed changes in administrative, academic, and support services.

8. **Anchor the Changes in the College's Culture.** Finally, to make any change stick, make it part of the college's mission. A first step is to place the change initiative into the institution's strategic plan. The president must talk about progress often. Create plans to replace key leaders of change if they move on. This will help ensure that their legacy is not lost or forgotten.

If community college leaders are to embark on a change initiative that is truly transformative, it is essential that all stakeholders get engaged in the process. Facilitating dialogue about the impact of organizational change is a major undertaking for the president and the senior leadership team. They must ensure that all stakeholders are appropriately included in the decision-making and change process. To engage stakeholders in organizational change conversations, leaders can arrange meetings in which stakeholders can come together to discuss the organizational challenges they face, while at the same time looking for sustainable solutions. The issues below are intended to stimulate discussions designed to provide an opportunity for the college community leaders to gather feedback and to review the perspectives of stakeholders by organizational changes.

Issues to Consider

A. How should a college leader instill pride in employees while also challenging them to improve outcomes?

B. A community college was placed on warning status by its regional accreditor for not having specified student-learning outcomes (SLOs) on file. The faculty association has taken the position that developing SLOs is not within the scope of faculty job descriptions, and that faculty should be paid extra for writing them. How should the college leadership deal with this issue?

C. Complete College America has called developmental education "the bridge to nowhere" because of its low success rates and the fact that very few students progress from developmental education to college-level coursework. Some states are limiting the number of developmental education courses that students can take. Other states are giving students the option of taking developmental education courses. Should community colleges admit students who have very low basic skills abilities? What can be done to improve student success rates in developmental education courses? Are there better ways to remediate basic skills weaknesses?

D. Major funding foundations are now supporting community college reform efforts. In the past, foundations, with a few exceptions, generally did not fund community colleges. What has caused this change? Is the foundation support helping or hindering the colleges? Can community colleges meet the goals set by President Obama, foundations, and community college associations?

E. Evaluations of the Achieving the Dream initiative have shown mixed results. What do you think are the factors that determine whether a college is going to be successful or not in improving student success rates?

F. AACC encourages community colleges to "redesign, reinvent, and reset (The 3 Rs)." Further, in the book, *Redesigning America's Community Colleges: A Clearer Path to Student Success* (Bailey et al., 2015), the authors suggest ways that community colleges should redesign academic programs for student success. How do you envision making the organizational changes at your college to respond to these challenges? What factors will need to be taken into consideration to make the changes? Which constituent groups will need to be engaged? What steps will need to be taken to engage them?

Case Scenario

You receive a memorandum from the chair of your college's English department informing you that the department faculty members have voted against scheduling classes at a neighboring military base because of the transient nature of the students, many of whom are deployed during the term. What issues does the scenario create? What leadership competencies are involved? Who should be involved in addressing this situation? What actions would you take? Are there lessons to be learned?

REFERENCES

Achieving the Dream. (2012). Building Institutional Capacity For Data-Informed Decision Making (Cutting Edge Series, No. 3). Retrieved from http://www.achievingthedream.org/_images/_index03/ukperfaccnt.pdf.

Alfred, R. L., & Carter, P. (1999). New Colleges for a New Century: Organizational Change and Development in Community Colleges. In J. Smart, (Ed.), *Higher Education: Handbook of Theory and Research* (Vol. 14, pp. 240–286). Bronx, NY: Agathon Press.

Alfred, R. L., Shults, C., Jaquette, O., & Strickland, S. (2009). *Community Colleges on the Horizon: Challenge, Choice, or Abundance?* American Council on Education Series on Higher Education. Lanham, MD: Rowman & Littlefield Education.

American Association of Community Colleges. (2010). College Completion Challenge: A Call to Action. Retrieved from: http://www.aacc.nche.edu/About/completionchallenge/Pages/default.aspx.

American Association of Community Colleges. (2012). *Reclaiming the American Dream: Community Colleges and the Nation's Future. A report of the 21st-Century Commission on the Future of Community Colleges.* Washington, DC: Author. Retrieved from: http://aacc.wpengine.com/wp-content/uploads/2014/03/21stCenturyReport.pdf.

American Association of Community Colleges. (2013). *AACC Competencies for Community College Leaders,* 2nd ed. Washington, DC: Author. Retrieved from: http://www.aacc.nche.edu/newsevents/Events/leadershipsuite/Documents/AACC_Core_Competencies_web.pdf.

American Association of Community Colleges. (2014). *Empowering Community Colleges to Build the Nation's Future: An Implementation Guide.* Washington, DC: Author. Retrieved from: http://www.aacc21stcenturycenter.org/wp-content/uploads/2014/04/EmpoweringCommunityColleges_final.pdf.

Amey, M. J., VanDerLinden, K. E., & Brown, D. F. (2002). Perspectives on Community College Leadership: Twenty Years in the Making. *Community College Journal of Research and Practice, 26, 573–589.*

Aune, B. P. (1995). The Human Dimension of Organizational Change. *Review of Higher Education, 18*(2), 149–173.

Bailey, T., Jaggars, S., & Jenkins, D. (2015). *Redesigning America's Community Colleges: A Clearer Path to Student Success.* Baltimore, MD: John Hopkins University Press.

Barrow, C. W. (1996). The Strategy of Selective Excellence: Redesigning Higher Education for Global Competition in a Postindustrial Society. *Higher Education, 31*(4), 447–469.

Benjamin, R., & Carroll, S. J. (1996). Impediments and Imperatives in Restructuring Higher Education. *Educational Administration Quarterly, 32,* 705–719.

Bichsel, J. (2012). *Analytics in Higher Education: Benefits, Barriers, Progress, and Recommendations* (Research Report). Louisville, CO: EDUCAUSE Center for Applied Research.

Bonk, C. J., & Graham, C. R. (2006). *The Handbook of Blended Learning Environments: Global Perspectives, Local Designs.* San Francisco, CA: Jossey-Bass/Pfeiffer.

Burke, W. W. (2011). *Organization Change: Theory and Practice* (3d ed.). Thousand Oaks, CA: Sage.

Burnes, B. (1996). *Managing Change: A Strategic Approach to Organizational Dynamics.* London: Pitman.

Burnett, D. J., & Oblinger, D. G. (Eds.). (2002). *Innovation in Student Services: Planning for Models Blending High Touch/High Tech.* Ann Arbor, MI: Society for College and University Planning.

Callan, P. (2006, Fall). Interview: Robert McCabe. National Cross Talk. National Center for Public Policy. Retrieved from: http://www.highereducation.org/crosstalk/ct1000/interview1000.shtml.

Cates, C., & Cedercreutz, K. (Eds.). (2008). *Leveraging Cooperative Education to Guide Curricular Innovation: The Development of a Corporate Feedback System for Continuous Improvement.* Cincinnati, OH: Center for Cooperative Education Research and Innovation.

Chermak, G. L. D. (1990). Cultural Dynamics: Principles to Guide Change in Higher Education. *College and University Professional Association for Human Resources, 41*(3), 25–27.

DeMers, C. (2007). *Organizational Change Theories: A Synthesis.* Thousand Oaks, CA: Sage.

Vincent, M., & Eisenstadt, T. (1998). *The Knowledge Web: Learning and Collaborating on the net, First Edition* (Open and Flexible Learning Series). New York, NY: Routledge.

Erwin, D. (1997). Developing Strategies and Policies for Changing Universities. In S. Armstrong, G. Thompson, & S. Brown (Eds.). *Facing Up to Radical Changes in Universities and Colleges* (pp. 64–73). London, UK: Kogan Press.

Floyd, D.L., Haley, A., Eddy, P.L. & Antczak, L. (2009). Celebrating the Past, Creating the Future: 50 Years of Community College Research. *Community College Journal of Research and Practice, 33*(3–4), 216–237.

Franklin, K. K. (2000). Shared and Connected Learning in a Freshman Learning Community. *Journal of First-Year Experience 12*(2), 33–63.

Gabriel, M. A. (2004). Learning Together: Exploring Group Interactions Online. *Journal of Distance Education 19*(1), 54–72.

Gardner, J. N., & Barefoot, B. O. (2011), *Your College Experience. Strategies for Success.* New York, NY: Macmillan.

Garrison, D. R., & Anderston, T. (2003). *E-learning in the 21st Century: Framework for Research and Practice.* London, UK: Rutledge Flamer.

Gesser, C. M. (2013). Using social media in the classroom: A community college perspective. *American Sociological Association Footnotes, 41*(1). Retrieved from http:// www.asanet.org/footnotes/jan13/ social_media_0113.html.

Gonzales, J. (2012, August 13). Real-Time Jobs Data Show Community College What Employers Need Now. *Chronicle of Higher Education.* Retrieved from: go.nmc.org/realda.

Gumport, P. J. (2000). Academic Restructuring: Organizational Change and Institutional Imperatives. *Higher Education, 39,* 67–91.

Hatcher, J. A., Bringle, R. G., & Muthiah, R. (2004). Designing Effective Reflection: What Matters to Service Learning? *Michigan Journal of Community Service Learning, 11*(1), 38–46. Retrieved from: http://quod. lib.umich.edu/cgi/t/text/pageviewer-idx?c=mjcsl;cc=mjcsl;rgn=full%20text; idno=3239521.0011.104;didno=3239521.0011.104;view=image; seq=00000001.

Hearn, J. C. (1996). Transforming U.S. Higher Education: An Organizational Perspective. *Innovative Higher Education, 21*(2), 141–154.

Howland, J. L., & Moore, J. (2002). Student Perceptions as Distance Learners in Internet-Based Courses. *Distance Education, 23*(2), 183–196.

Jacobs, J., & Dougherty, K. J. (2006). The Uncertain Future of the Community College Workforce Development Mission. *New Directions for Community Colleges, 2006, 53–62.* doi: 10.1002/cc.259.

Katzenbach, J. (2003). *Why Pride Matters More Than Money.* New York, NY: Crown Business.

Kim, W. C., & Mauborgne, R. A. (2003). Tipping Point Leadership. *Harvard Business Review, 81*(4), 60–69.

Kotter, J. P. (1995). *The New Rules: How to Succeed in Today's Post-corporate World.* New York, NY: Free Press.

Kotter, J. P. (1997). Leading Change: A Conversation with John P. Kotter. *Strategy & Leadership, 25*(1), 18–23.

Kotter, J. (2008). *A Sense of Urgency.* Boston, MA: Harvard Business Press.

Levine L. J., & Shapiro, N. (2004). *Sustaining and Improving Learning Communities.* San Francisco, CA: Jossey-Bass

Lewin, K. M. (2007, June). *Improving Access, Equity and Transitions in Education: Creating a Research Agenda* (Create Pathways to Access Research Monograph No. 1). Retrieved from http://www.create-rpc.org/pdf_documents/PTA1.pdf.

Ludwig-Hardman, S., & Dunlap, J. (2003). Learner Support Services for Online Students: Scaffolding for Success. *International Review of Research in Open and Distributed Learning, 4*(1). Retrieved from http://www.irrodl.org/index.php/irrodl/article/view/131/602.

Maginn, M. (2005). *Managing in Times of Change.* San Francisco, CA: McGraw-Hill.

Mallen, M. J., Vogel, D. L., Rochlen, A. B., & Day, S. X. (2005). Online counseling: Reviewing the literature from a counseling psychology framework. *The counseling Pychologist. 33*(6), 819–871.

McCabe, R. (2000). *Underprepared Students. Measuring Up 2000: The State by State Report Card for Higher Education.* Retrieved from: http://measuringup.highereducation.org/2000/articles/UnderpreparedStudents.cfm.

MDRC. (2013). *Developmental Education: A Barrier to a Postsecondary Credential for Millions of Americans.* Retrieved from http://www.mdrc.org/sites/default/files/Dev%20Ed_020113.pdf.

Phelan, D. J. (2016). *Unrelenting Change, Disruptive Innovation and Risk: Forging the Next Generation of Community Colleges.* Lanham, MD: Rowman & Littlefield.

Savage, R. N. (2007, June 24–27). *A Design Methodology for Empowering Project-Based Learning* (AC2007–3119). Proceedings of the 2007 ASEE Annual Conference "Riding the Wave to Excellence in Engineering Education." Honolulu, HI.

Senge, P. (2008). *The Necessary Revolution: How Individuals and Organizations Are Working Together to Create a Sustainable World*. New York, NY: Doubleday.

Simpson, O. (2002). *Supporting Students in Open and Distance Learning* (2nd ed.). London, UK: Kogan.

Stober, D. (2008). Making It Stick: Coaching as a Tool for Organizational Change. *Journal of Theory, Research and Practice, 1*(1), 71–80.

Stone, M. E., & Jacobs, G. (Eds.). (2008). *Supplemental Instruction: Improving First-Year Student Success in High-Risk Courses* (Monograph No. 7, 3rd ed.). Columbia, SC: University of South Carolina, National Resource Center for The First-Year Experience and Students in Transition.

Strebel, P. (2006). Why Do Employees Resist Change? *Harvard Business Press Review, 11*(1), 45–62.

Tagg, J. (2012). Why Does the Faculty Resist Change? *Change, 44*(1), 6–15.

Van de Ven, A. H., & Poole, M. (1995). Explaining Development and Change in Organizations. *Academy of Management Review, 20*(3), 510–540.

Vincent, M., & Eisenstadt, T. (1998). *The Knowledge Web: Learning and Collaborating on the Net, First Edition* (Open and Flexible Learning Series). New York, NY: Routledge.

Waters, J. K. (2014, April 14). *The Great Adaptive Learning Experiment*. (1105 Media Inc.) Retrieved from http://campustechnology.com/Articles/2014/04/16/The-Great-Adaptive-Learning-Experiment.aspx.

Watson, L. W., Williams, F. K., & Derby, D. C. (2005, Spring). Contemporary Multicultural Issues: Student, Faculty, and Administrator Perceptions. *Community College Enterprise, 11*(1), 79–92.

Weick, K. E. (1995). *Sense Making in Organizations*. Thousand Oaks, CA: Sage.

Wu, M. (2012, October 9). *Gamification 101: The Psychology of Motivation*. Retrieved from http://lithosphere.lithium.com/t5/science-of-social-blog/Gamification-101-The-Psychology-of-Motivation/ba-p/21864.

8

SAFETY AND SECURITY

Responsibility for Safety and Security

There are 1,167 public and independent community colleges—1,600 when branch campuses are included in the count (American Association of Community Colleges [AACC, 2015]). Because of an increasing number of violent crimes, natural disasters, and other emergencies or crises, many of the leaders of these colleges are convening committees and task forces to reexamine or conduct a comprehensive review of policies, procedures, and systems related to campus safety and security (Foster, 2007; Redden, 2008). The Crime Awareness and Campus Security Act of 1990 legislated requirements for colleges and universities to develop policies and procedures to provide a safe campus environment and to keep students, parents, and employees well informed about campus security. The federal Jeanne Clery Act of 1998 requires institutions to issue timely warnings to the campus community and to report crimes considered to be a threat to students and employees. It is essential that community college leaders possess the knowledge and skills to ensure that their institutions are in full compliance with federal and state requirements (Pelletier, 2008; Ward & Mann, 2011).

In previous chapters of this book, we identified a wide range of issues and challenges that relate to leadership in the community college environment. We acknowledged the complex structures and changing demographics of community colleges that present a unique set of circumstances that must be considered when leadership issues are examined. Likewise, there is no "cookie-cutter" or "one-size-fits-all" solution for community colleges to address issues of safety and security. Specifically, community colleges' student populations change from term to term, and many institutions rely on a large number of part-time employees that changes from term to term and from year to year. In addition to their onsite facilities, many community colleges offer programs and services at locations off campus that cover a wide range of geographical locations. The different locations coupled with changing demographics pose myriad safety and security challenges, including issues involving access to facilities, surveillance, and staffing and resource allocation. Robin Hattersley Gray, in a June 13, 2014, article in *Campus Safety* magazine, stated that 95 percent of campus presidents do not want guns on their campuses, even though some states have passed legislation to authorize them and others are considering it. Although the issue of guns on campus and whether their presence makes a campus safer or less safe is debatable, Hattersley Gray identified some important issues related to gun violence in this article.

> An examination found the five most common campus safety measures were: identifying and referring potentially violent students to appropriate services (91%), mass text alerts (91%), active shooter plan (85%), campus police presence (82%) and video cameras (77%). However, less than half of the presidents indicated either their faculty (45%) or their student body (38%) was trained to respond to an active shooter on campus. (Gray, 2014)

Community college leaders have a responsibility to address issues like those that might be caused by guns in college facilities and to ensure the safety and security of those stakeholders on their campuses. They need to provide leadership for the development of appropriate policies, procedures, and strategies to maintain a safe campus (Midwestern Higher Education Compact, 2008).

Commitment and Enforcement

Despite the ongoing complexity of the many issues faced by community college leaders, those relating to emergency preparedness and campus security and safety should not be assigned a lower priority to be addressed at some later date. Today, safety and security are front and center of the day-to-day issues in higher education (Lipka, 2009). Lipka argues that reported crime numbers imply certainty, and when it comes to campus crime, everybody wants answers. She explains that although the Clery Act set out to reveal the crimes that take place on campus, there is wide variability in how colleges report data, and there are contradictory interpretations by prospective and current students, administrators, and the media on what the data mean. Given these problems, community college leaders must be committed to fostering environments that make the enforcement of the Clery Act and the accurate reporting of crime statistics top priorities at their institutions. Presidential leadership, in particular, is essential in developing and maintaining up-to-date emergency preparedness and campus and security management plans. The president's acting as chief advocate for campus safety and security is critical to effective management of these issues.

Although there has been a plethora of recent incidents and reports about natural disasters, crimes, and violence on college campuses, very little has been written about the specific role that community college leaders have defined for themselves in designing and implementing plans to address these issues. This omission suggests that safety and security management needs to be more visible and closely integrated into the culture of the institution and an important component of the leadership duties of the president and other campus leaders.

So, what should a president do to provide leadership for safety and security management? Creating a safe and secure community requires the involvement of all stakeholders. The president must create an environment in which stakeholders are able to work together to mitigate the consequences of crimes, natural disasters, and other hazards. Planning and preparing prompt and deliberate responses to these situations and establishing the means to help the campus recover are all important aspects of the leaders' jobs (International Association of Emergency Managers, 2007). Failure to have an up-to-date emergency preparedness plan in place and to provide related ongoing staff development and training could disqualify a college from receiving government support to rebuild after a disaster.

In the wake of the recent violence in the United States and Europe, college and university officials throughout the United States are increasingly being asked to remind their constituencies of resources and efforts designed to keep students, faculty, and staff safe at all campuses (Foster, 2007; Lipka, 2009; National Association of College and University Attorneys, 2007). Although there were previous instances of campus violence, the Virginia Tech shootings on April 16, 2007, which claimed the lives of thirty-two students and faculty, called attention to the responsibilities of leadership in ways that no previous incident had. An investigation by the Department of Education (which is responsible for enforcing the Clery Act) reported the following finding on December 9, 2010: Virginia Tech failed to comply with the timely warning issuance and policy provisions of the Clery Act. No one knows whether timely alerts by Virginia Tech would have resulted in fewer casualties, and people are still debating about what could have been done to prevent the October 2015 massacre at Umpqua College in Oregon, where a twenty-six-year-old man opened fire on campus in a rampage that left ten people dead and seven wounded. However, we do know that there are many lessons to be learned from the Virginia Tech and the Umpqua stories. Community college leaders should study and learn from each safety and security incident as they work toward creating and maintaining safe and secure environments on their campuses. Suttel (2006) suggested that institutions must pay increased attention to building security. "Instituting a new security management plan or beefing up an existing plan will only enhance a facility's safety level." Although elements will vary depending on building type and function, every building security program assessment should examine three key focus areas:

1. What physical systems are in place?
2. How are the systems being applied to effectively provide operational security?
3. Are security systems and procedures being explained correctly and clearly to employees and students? Are they given appropriate training?

Although community college leaders must be concerned about safety and security issues, they also have to be aware of the need to balance institutional security with student privacy. Valuable information about this delicate balance is explained in a US Department of Education publication entitled *Balancing Student Privacy and School Safety: A Guide to the Family Educational Rights and Privacy Act for Colleges and Universities* (2008a). Community college leaders are encouraged to use this information to stimulate conversation and to launch appropriate security and safety management plans at their institutions.

Truth and Consequences of Crime Reporting

The Jeanne Clery Disclosure of Campus Security Policy and Campus Crime Statistics Act (Clery Act, 2008) is a federal statute, and compliance is not optional for any college or university that receives federal funds. The law is named after Jeanne Clery, a nineteen-year-old Lehigh University student who was raped and murdered in her campus residence hall in 1986. Her murder triggered a backlash against unreported crime on campuses across the country. Community college leaders must understand both the rationale for the regulations and the consequences for noncompliance. For instance, community colleges that participate in federal financial aid programs must keep and disclose information about crime on and adjacent to their campuses. When colleges are found to be in a noncompliance status, there may be penalties up to $35,000 per violation, and the college may be suspended from participating in federal student financial aid programs.

President Barack Obama signed the Violence Against Women Reauthorization Act (VAWA) into law on March 7, 2013. Section 304 of VAWA amended section 485(f) of the Higher Education Act (Clery Act). In addition to clarifying and making technical revisions to the Clery Act, VAWA significantly expanded reporting requirements to include incidents of dating violence, domestic violence, and stalking. VAWA also enhanced the policies, procedures, and programs institutions must include related to these incidents.

Title IX of the 1972 Federal Education Amendments requires colleges and universities receiving federal funding to combat gender-based violence and harassment and to respond to the needs of survivors in order to ensure that all students have equal access to education. Although any college employee may report incidents of gender-based violence or harassment for investigation, several classifications of employees have been identified as "mandatory reporters" for Title IX purposes. These employees have authority and responsibility to take action to remedy and report gender-based issues. Examples of mandatory reporters include senior administrators, deans, directors, supervisors, department heads, faculty members, coaches, and student affairs professionals. Students have used Title IX to file successful federal complaints or civil lawsuits against colleges.

Community college leaders must be aware of the college's reporting requirements. The annual crime statistics report is due by October 1 of each year and must be published and made available to employees and current and prospective students. Community college presidents should routinely review the report with the staff members responsible for compiling it. All too often, community college leaders are not only unaware of the report, but they also have no knowledge of their college's crime statistics. Leaders also need to be aware of the fact that the crime report must include crime statistics for the prior three years along with college policy statements regarding safety and security measures. Leaders must take this report seriously and carefully monitor it so that all compliance aspects are followed, including the investigation and appropriate prosecution of alleged sexual offenses. Although community college leaders are not expected to be criminal justice experts, they are encouraged to become knowledgeable of the basic requirements so that they can be in the position to effectively monitor issues that involve alleged criminal issues.

For example, presidents can ask questions of the college security office or police department, such as, is the college's crime log up to date? The law requires the crime log to have the most recent sixty days of information, and each log must contain the nature, date, time, and general location of each crime and how that crime was investigated and resolved. Further, the presidents must be knowledgeable of the procedures that their colleges use to provide timely warnings of any crime that represents a threat to the safety of students or employees. College leaders need to ensure that polices regarding timely warnings are included in the annual campus security report and reviewed with employees and students in a transparent manner. According to the statute, institutions are required to report on crimes such as murder, sexual offenses, aggravated assault, robbery, vehicle theft, arson, liquor law violations, illegal weapon possession, and drug-related offenses. It is natural for college leaders to want to protect the reputation of their colleges, and they may be concerned that reporting crime data might negatively affect the image of the college. However, transparency is the best policy. Community college leaders must continue to be aggressive in creating victim friendly cultures that encourage students to report crimes to police or campus officials. The objective is to make the campus safer for students and employees.

Leadership Practices for Safety and Security Management

On December 6, 2015, President Obama addressed the nation on his top priority: keeping Americans safe. He said, "As Commander-in-Chief, I have no greater responsibility than the security of the American people" (White House, 2015). Community college leaders must adopt a similar position pertaining to their colleges—the highest priority for the community college president must be the safety and well-being of students, faculty, and staff. The National Integration Center's National Incident Management System (NIMS) Integration Division (http://www.fema.gov/emergency/nims) is an excellent resource for leaders to learn more about security and crime incident reporting in higher education. It is clear that many community colleges already have a number of programs in place to help individuals become more aware of safety and security issues (Midwestern Higher Education Compact, 2008; International Association of Campus Law Enforcement Administrators, 2008). To help facilitate a better understanding of what leaders can do to foster a safe and secure campus environment, we offer a few suggestions for college leaders:

1. Demonstrate Leadership Commitment

Effective safety and security management begins with the senior leadership (Ward & Mann, 2011). The president of the college must initiate and support safety and security efforts to ensure engagement from the entire campus community. The president has the decision-making power and the authority to devote resources to implement a safety and security initiative and subsequently put into action the plans to provide for the welfare of the campus. The president has the authority to allocate fiscal and human resources to support safety and security efforts. It is important to have high-level support to provide both political and financial backing to promote the safety and security effort. Leaders are encouraged to integrate the safety and security work into other appropriate college plans to ensure that it is institutionalized.

2. Assess Culture and Climate

Reviewing existing campus and community data is an important responsibility of college leaders. It is a good idea to review previous vulnerability assessments of the institution and surrounding community as well as related facility safety and security assessments. *A Guide to Vulnerability Assessments: Key Principles for Safe Schools* (2008b), a US Department of Education publication, can be used for suggestions and strategies to enhance assessment of safety and security issues at colleges.

3. Conduct an Inventory of Resources

Leaders should become knowledgeable about the existing safety and security resources on their campuses and in the community. This task will take time, and leaders may have to rely on other staff members or groups to support this effort. It is important for presidents to designate a senior staff member to assume oversight responsibility for safety and security in order for the campus community to recognize its importance. The president must also identify those departments that must play a significant role in preparing for, responding to, and recovering from a crisis or emergency situation. Through these actions, the president can demonstrate commitment and leadership for safety and security on campus (International Association of Emergency Managers, 2007).

4. Develop and Implement a Safety and Security Plan

Presidents must take the necessary action to ensure that the emergency preparedness and safety and security management plans are part of the college's core values and are incorporated into the comprehensive strategic plan of the institution. The president is uniquely positioned to use the authority of the office to promote the college's safety and security initiatives. In 2007, the US Department of Education released a document entitled *Practical Information on Crisis Planning*, which contains ideas for building a safety and security management plan. Similar to other institutional effectiveness initiatives, the unique aspects of the campus environment, such as campus size, geographic location of the campus, number and type of buildings, community resources, and student demographics, must be taken into consideration in safety and security planning.

5. Establish a Strategic Communication Process

A safety and security initiative requires clear lines of communication. The CEO must work with the leadership team and other administrators to ensure that every department on campus assumes responsibility for creating a safe environment. It is also important for the CEO to build and maintain meaningful internal and external partnerships to sustain effective safety and security efforts. These partnerships include faculty and student organizations, community groups (such as law enforcement, fire safety, health and mental health organizations), media, and community organizations (US Department of Education, 2008a, 2011). The communication process should be ongoing and must be incorporated into the way the college conducts its business.

6. Support Professional Development and Training

College leaders need to establish policies that require professional development and training for institutional employees on the college's safety and security initiatives. Trainings and exercises must be incorporated into the culture of the college and not be considered a one-time or periodic event that takes place sporadically or in a reactive manner after a crisis has occurred. Training must emphasize the protocols and procedures in the safety and security management plan and should include simulations and tabletop exercises. Professional development training is an excellent way to tap into the expertise of faculty and community partners. The president has an obligation to ensure that adequate funding for security and safety management and training appears in the college's budget on an annual basis.

7. Disseminate Safety and Security Messages

It is not enough to simply develop a safety and security management plan. Information about the plan must be disseminated to students, staff, faculty, and community partners. The president and leadership team must take action to ensure that safety and security plans are visibly displayed on the institution's website and in buildings throughout the campus. According to EDUCAUSE (2008), the role of information technology in campus security and emergency management is continuing to evolve. We encourage existing and emerging leaders to seek ways to remain current in the use of technology and other resources that can be utilized to inform the college community about safety and security issues on campus. The president should hold appropriate campus administrators responsible for routinely reviewing safety and security plans with students, staff, faculty, and all of the varied campus support personnel so they are prepared to respond in an emergency. Finally, the leadership team can take action to test and practice the plan in training sessions on a routine basis (US Department of Education, 2011).

Key Safety and Security Management Leadership Questions

It is important for presidents and other senior leadership team members to make informed decisions about safety and security management plans and related activities and programs. The following key questions can serve as motivation for collecting qualitative data that can be used to institutionalize safety and security management programs:

1. What actions have been taken, and what actions still need to be taken to minimize the potential for campus violence?
2. Who is responsible for crisis prevention and response on campus? Are responsibilities clearly assigned?
3. What professional development and training activities has the college sponsored in order minimize the potential for crises and to respond effectively to it?
4. What relevant legislation should the president and the leadership team be aware of?
5. Does the college have an emergency preparedness or safety and security management plan? Is the plan up to date? Are employees aware of the plan?
6. What is the college's communication plan in case of disaster or other campus crisis? Who is responsible for communications?

7. Is the college in compliance with the reporting of crime statistics as required by federal and state laws?

8. What partnerships are in place that can support the college's safety and security initiatives? Does the college have agreements with all of the appropriate community partners to support the efforts? Are these agreements up to date?

The president and leadership team can use these questions to enrich the safety and security narrative and to jump-start conversations about security and safety concerns at the college.

Resources

All of us dread the potential for having to deal with a crisis, especially if it results in tragic loss of life, injury, or significant damage to a college campus. Unfortunately, these incidents have become more common. What would be even more dreadful in these situations is if college leaders are not prepared or respond inappropriately. This chapter on safety and security management offers some suggestions for leaders to consider in addressing issues related to emergency preparedness and safety and security. Senior leadership's commitment and support within the institution is critical to the success of safety and security efforts. As discussed, college presidents must make safety and security a top priority among their leadership goals.

Leaders and aspiring leaders must take individual responsibility for obtaining and maintaining up-to-date safety and security management resources. Community colleges are places of teaching and learning; it is only appropriate that a spirit of learning and information sharing should be reflected in the emergency management planning process. Recent campus tragedies are shocking reminders of the need for community colleges to be ready to activate a comprehensive campus-wide safety and security plan with procedures for coordinating responses and recovery activities.

The US Departments of Education and Justice provide publications, programs, and resources to assist college leaders to plan appropriately for campus emergencies.

1. The Emergency Management for Higher Education (EMHE)
   Grant Program. This program supports institutions of higher
   education (IHE) projects designed to develop, or review and
   improve, and fully integrate campus-based, all-hazards emergency
   management planning efforts.

2. *The Action Guide for Emergency Management at Institutions of Higher Education.* This guide (US Department of Education, 2010) can help personnel from higher education institutions and their partners better understand the field of emergency management within a higher education context, develop and implement an institution's emergency management plan, and serve as a reference and resource to improve an institution's existing plans. The revised *Action Guide* is not meant to serve as a prescriptive document but rather is intended to provide a number of resources and references to facilitate the emergency management planning process for institutions at all levels of knowledge and development.

3. *The Handbook for Campus Safety and Security Reporting.* This handbook from the Department of Education (Ward & Mann, 2011) is intended to familiarize the reader with the amended Clery Act and the new regulations that were added by the Higher Education Opportunity Act (HEOA). The 2011 edition takes readers step by step along the path to compliance and explains what the regulations mean and what they require of institutions.

4. *Balancing Student Privacy and School Safety: A Guide to the Family Educational Rights and Privacy Act for Colleges and Universities.* This publication (US Department of Education, 2008a) provides guidance pertaining to the Family Educational Rights and Privacy Act (FERPA), disciplinary records, the Clery Act, law enforcement units, disclosure to parents, and other information that will help campus officials make decisions quickly when confronted with issues about privacy and safety.

5. The Readiness and Emergency Management for Schools (REMS) Technical Assistance (TA) Center. This center supports K–12 schools, colleges, and universities in providing emergency management resources, training, and publications for improving and strengthening their emergency management plans through the provision of resources, responses to technical assistance requests, and facilitation of Emergency Management for Schools Training events.

6. Family Policy Compliance Office. This office within the US Department of Education implements the Family Educational Rights and Privacy Act (FERPA) and the Protection of Pupil Rights Amendment (PPRA). Parents and eligible students who

need assistance or wish to file a complaint under FERPA or PPRA should do so in writing to the Family Policy Compliance Office.

7. Travel Warnings and Consular Information Sheets. Should a student consider studying in a foreign country, the US Department of Education suggests that he or she visit this Department of State website (https://travel.state.gov/content/passports/en/country.html) prior to making a final decision.

8. FBI Crime Reporting Systems. Information on crime in the United States can be obtained at the Federal Bureau of Investigation's website (https://www.fbi.gov/report-threats-and-crime).

9. US Department of Justice, Office on Violence Against Women. Information and resources are available from the Department of Justice's Violence Against Women Office (http://www.justice.gov/ovw) to stop domestic violence, sexual assault, and stalking. Information is also provided about grants to reduce violent crimes against women on campus.

10. US Department of Justice, COPS Program. The Community Oriented Policing Services (COPS) grant program makes funds available for a number of safety and security purposes. Postsecondary institutions can use funds to strengthen security (http://eric.ed.gov/?id=ED442338/).

11. Education's Higher Education Center for Alcohol and Other Drug Prevention. The center is the nation's primary resource center for assisting higher education institutions in the development, implementation, and evaluation of alcohol and drug violence prevention policies and programs that foster students' academic and social development and promote campus and community safety (http://www.campushealthandsafety.org/resources/resource_rws_225.html).

12. *The Federal Student Aid Handbook.* The *FSA Handbook* describes the consumer information, including the campus security, requirements that an institution must provide to students, the US Department of Education, and others (https://studentaid.ed.gov/sa/).

The staff member appointed by the college president to be responsible for safety and security issues should be aware of the laws governing these issues.

UNITED STATES DEPARTMENT OF LABOR: OCCUPATIONAL SAFETY & HEALTH ADMINISTRATION (OSHA) CODE OF FEDERAL REGULATIONS

1. An employer must have a written Emergency Action Plan (29 CFR 1910.38)
2. An employer must have a written Fire Prevention Plan (29 CFR 1910.39)

CODE OF FEDERAL REGULATIONS

○ Title 44: Emergency Management and Assistance
○ Critical Infrastructure Security and Resilience
○ Critical Infrastructure Protection

UNITED STATES CODE

○ Robert T. Stafford Disaster Relief and Emergency Assistance Act (42 USC Section 5121): Statutory authority for Federal disaster response (FEMA)
○ Homeland Security Act of 2002: Critical Infrastructure Information Act (6 USC 131–134)
○ Jeanne Clery Disclosure of Campus Security Policy & Campus Crime Statistics Act (20 USC 1092(f))

PUBLIC LAW: ADMINISTRATION OF DISASTER RELIEF

○ The Federal Disaster Relief Act of 1950 (P.L. 81–875)
○ Disaster Relief Act of 1966 (P.L. 89–769)
○ Disaster Relief Act of 1974 (P.L. 93–288)
○ The Robert T. Stafford Disaster Relief and Emergency Assistance Act (P.L. 93–288)
○ Post-Katrina Emergency Management Reform Act of 2006 (P.L. 109–295)

HOMELAND SECURITY PRESIDENTIAL DIRECTIVES (HSPD)

○ HSPD-5: Directive on Management of Domestics Incidents— Requires federally funded programs to comply with the National Incident Management System (NIMS) o HSPD-7: Critical Infrastructure Identification, Prioritization, and Protection—Roles of federal, state, and local agencies receiving funding

o HSPD-8: National preparedness of all levels of government and the private and nonprofit sectors

HIGHER EDUCATION OPPORTUNITY ACT (HEOA)

o Campus Safety Requirements: Institutions of Higher Education to have NIMS compliant emergency operations plans and to practice them annually

NATIONAL FIRE PROTECTION ASSOCIATION

o NFPA 1600: Standard for Emergency Management and Business Continuity Programs

Athletics

Athletic participation is an important part of higher education for many students. For some students, it may be the principle motivation for going to college, and participation can teach important skills about teamwork and personal effort. But there is an increased awareness of safety, especially in sports in which repetitive injury can cause permanent disability or even death. It is essential that college leaders communicate with student-athletes and coaches at the beginning of each term that injuries, especially concussions, must be treated with the primary objective of student-athlete safety. This directive also should be clearly visible in student-athlete handbooks, coaches' handbooks, and websites (National Collegiate Athletic Association, 2015).

Cybersecurity Issues

As community colleges have become increasingly reliant on technology, they have become more vulnerable to cyberattacks and thefts of sensitive data. News reports of data breaches that affect customers of major businesses and retail stores have become common. Higher education is, of course, not immune to this threat and the issues created by a breach in security of information technology systems. Katie Beautin (2015, p. 695) reminds us that colleges and universities store a vast amount of private information on students and employees, including educational and medical records. She points out that there have been more than seven hundred publically recorded data breaches involving educational institutions between 2005 and 2014.

How institutions prepare for and respond to cybersecurity attacks and loss of data will determine how vulnerable they will be to litigation and government actions. Unfortunately, not enough colleges are planning effectively to reduce the damage that can be done by a cybercrime. The costs incurred by an institution in response to a data breach can be substantial. Expenses can include forensics consultants, lawyers, call centers, websites, mailings, identity protection and credit check services, and litigation (Beautin, 2015, p. 688).

Colleges and universities are in a unique position in that they are subject to multiple federal and state statutes regulating data privacy, including consumer reporting laws, the Family Educational Rights and Privacy Act (FERPA), and the Health Insurance Portability and Accountability Act (HIPPA). In addition, they can face class action lawsuits and Federal Trade Commission (FTC) action in the wake of a cyberbreach (Beautin, 2015, p. 659). Insurance against these kinds of threats is expensive and difficult to obtain (p. 689).

Cybersecurity is vulnerable to several different kinds of threats—from hackers, who find weaknesses in computer networks and then install malware to gain access, to thefts of insecure laptops or other portable devices that lack encryption, to criminal activity on the part of employees or former employees. Motivations include personal financial gain by selling information, revenge for a perceived wrongdoing, or changes to student grade records.

In March 2013, hackers accessed a database of student admissions records at Kirkwood Community College in Cedar Rapids, Iowa (Beautin, 2015, p. 666). The college responded by hiring an outside firm to do a forensic analysis of the breach and offering credit monitoring to affected individuals (Data FAQs, 2013). In April 2013, the Maricopa Community College District in Arizona experienced a large-scale data breach involving nearly 2.5 million employees and current and former students. The compromised information included employee social security numbers, driver's license numbers, bank account information, and student academic records (Beautin, 2015, p. 682). The victims of the breach filed a class action complaint against the District on April 14, 2014. By December 17, 2014, the cost to the Maricopa Community College District had exceeded $26 million (Faller, 2014).

The Maricopa Community College District Information Security Services Office (October 2014) offers some valuable advice to limit vulnerability to a cyber attack in its posting, *31 Days of Cyber Security Tips*. Some of the most important messages to communicate to employees include:

1. USB (flash) drives and other external devices can be infected by viruses and malware. If they are needed, use your security software to scan them before use.
2. Protect all devices that are connected to the Internet (computers, laptops, smartphones, and other Web-enabled devices).
3. Practice good password management. Use a strong mix of characters, do not share your password with others, and do not write it down and leave it on or near your computer.
4. Download applications and ringtones with caution. Some may come with a virus attached.
5. Do not open unknown attachments.
6. Do not click on unknown links.
7. Use a privacy screen when traveling.
8. Refrain from using an unsecured Wi-Fi network when traveling.
9. Back up your data regularly.
10. Make sure your antivirus software is up to date.

Community college leaders need to become more aware of the potential for cyberattacks and data breaches and to institute policies and procedures that minimize risk. Leaders also should think in advance about the issues involved in a data breach and how the college should respond appropriately.

Issues to Consider

A. What can colleges do to improve the safety and security of students and staff? How should colleges handle reports of sexual assault?
B. One person was killed and two others were injured on the afternoon of September 3, 2015, during a shooting in a Sacramento City College campus parking lot. It took 44 minutes to send an alert to students through the school's WARN messaging system. The person in charge admitted he couldn't log into the system because "he could not remember the decoy letters on the logon code" (Sangree, 2015). How can problems like this one be prevented?

C. On November 19, 2015, a female Muslim student at San Diego State University reported that an unknown man pushed her and pulled her by her headscarf while making "hate-related comments and threats based on her ethnicity" (Altman, 2015). What steps should college leaders take to respond to an incident like this? Are there some actions that college leaders should take to minimize the potential for these kinds of incidents?

D. "Campus carry" laws, permitting eligible students and employees to carry lethal weapons on campuses have been enacted in several states, and other states are considering legislation either to allow weapons on campuses or to ban them. Do laws that allow guns make campuses safer or less safe? Are there some places on campus where guns should not be allowed?

E. What steps should your college leadership take to minimize vulnerability to cyberattacks and data breaches?

Case Scenario

Your Chief of Campus Security calls you to tell you that he has received a call from a female student who has been threatened by her husband. The student is in the nursing program and has been pressured by her husband to drop out and stay home to take care of him and the children. He has abused her in the past and has thrown out her books and homework assignments. Because of the physical abuse, she and her children separated from the husband and moved into subsidized housing. However, he has continued to try to get her to move "home." Last evening, he called to tell her that, if she went to class today, he would come on campus and shoot her dead. The student is afraid he will follow through with his threat. Campus Security is concerned for the safety of this student and others who might get in the way of a gun-wielding husband. What issues does the scenario create? What leadership competencies are involved? Who should be involved in addressing the situation? What actions would you take? Are there lessons to be learned?

REFERENCES

Altman, J. (2015, November 23). Police Investigating Hate Crime Against
    Muslim San Diego State Univ. student. *USA Today*. Retrieved from:
    http://college.usatoday.com/2015/11/23/hate-crime-against-muslim-
    sdsu-student/.
American Association of Community Colleges. (2015). *Fast Facts*. Retrieved
    from: http://www.aacc.nche.edu/AboutCC/Pages/fastfactsfactsheet.aspx.
Beautin, K. (2015). College and University Data Breaches: Regulating Higher
    Education Cybersecurity Under State and Federal Law. *Journal of
    College and University Law,* 41(3). Retrieved from http://www.nacua.
    org/securedocuments/nonsearched/jcul/41_jcul_657.pdf.
Data FAQs. (2013). Kirkwood Community College. Retrieved from: http://
    www.kirkwood.edu/datafaqs.
EDUCAUSE. (2008, October). *The Role of IT in Campus Security and Emergency
    Management*. Retrieved from: http://net.educause.edu/ir/library/pdf/
    pub9001.pdf.
Faller, M. B. (2014, December 17). Maricopa County Colleges Computer Hack
    Cost Tops $26M. *Arizona Republic*. Retrieved from: http://www.azcentral.
    com/story/news/local/phoenix/2014/12/17/costs-repair-massive-mcccd-
    computer-hack-top-million/20539491/.
Foster, A. (2007). After Va. Tech, Campuses Rush to Add Alert Systems.
    Chronicle of Higher Education. Retrieved from: http://chronicle.com/
    article/After-Va-Tech-Campuses-Rush/9259.
Gray, R. H. (2014, June 13). Presidents Don't Want Guns on Their Campuses.
    Campus Safety. Retrieved from: http://www.campussafetymagazine.com/
    article/95_of_college_presidents_dont_want_guns_on_campus/research.
International Association of Campus Law Enforcement Administrators. (2008).
    Campus Preparedness Resource Center. Retrieved from: http://www.iaclea.
    org/ visitors/wmdcpt/cprc/aboutcprc.cfm.
International Association of Emergency Managers. (2007, September 11).
    Principles of Emergency Management. Retrieved from: http://www.iaem.
    com/publications/documents/EMPrinciples091107.pdf.
Jeanne Clery Disclosure of Campus Security Policy and Campus Crime Statistics
    Act. (2008). Retrieved from: http://www.securityoncampus.org/index.
    php?option=com_content&view=art icle&id=271&Itemid=60 (accessed
    Jan. 1, 2009).
Lipka, S. (2009, January 30). In Campus-Crime Reports, There Is Little Safety in
    Numbers. *Chronicle of Higher Education*. Retrieved from: http://chronicle.
    com/article/In-Campus-Crime-Reports/30058.

Maricopa Community College District Information Security Services Office.
    (October 2014). *31 Days of Cyber Security Tips*. Retrieved from: https://
    its.maricopa.edu/infosec/31-days-of-cyber-security-tips.
Midwestern Higher Education Compact. (2008, May). *The Ripple Effect of
    Virginia Tech: Assessing the Nationwide Impact on Campus Safety and
    Security Policy and Practice*. Retrieved from http://files.eric.ed.gov/fulltext/
    ED502232.pdf.
National Association of College and University Attorneys. (2007, August).
    NOTES on FERPA and Campus Safety, 5(4). Retrieved from:
    http://www.nacua.org/ documents/ferpa2.pdf.
National Collegiate Athletic Association. (2015). *Concussion Guidelines*.
    Retrieved from: http://www.ncaa.org/health-and-safety/concussion-
    guidelines.
Pelletier, S. (2008). Campus Security Under the Microscope. *AGB Trusteeship,
    16*(3), 9–12.
Redden, E. (2008, April 7). Predicting and Preventing Campus Violence.
    InsideHigherEd.com. Retrieved from: http://www.insidehighered.com/
    news/2008/04/07/violence.
Sangree, H. (2015, October 25). Sacramento City College shooting still has
    campus rattled. *Sacramento Bee*. Retrieved from: http://www.sacbee.com/
    news/local/crime/article41399610.html.
Suttell, R. (2006). Security: A Blueprint for Reducing Risk. *Buildings, 100*(2),
    34–39.
US Department of Education, National Center for Education Statistics.
    (2006). *Digest of Education Statistics*. Retrieved from: http://nces.ed.
    gov/programs/digest/.
US Department of Education. (2007, January). *Practical Information on Crisis
    Planning: A Guide for Schools and Communities* (Revised). Retrieved
    from: http://www.ed.gov/ emergency plan/.
US Department of Education. (2008a). *Balancing Student Privacy and School
    Safety: A Guide to the Family Educational Rights and Privacy Act for
    Colleges and Universities*. Retrieved from: http://www.ed.gov/policy/gen/
    guid/fpco/brochures/postsec.pdf.
US Department of Education. (2008b). *A Guide to Vulnerability Assessments:
    Key Principles for Safe Schools*. Retrieved from: https://rems.ed.gov/docs/
    VA_Report_2008.pdf.
US Department of Education. (2010). *Action Guide for Emergency Management
    at Institutions of Higher Education*. Retrieved from: http://rems.ed.gov/
    docs/REMS_ActionGuide.pdf.

US Department of Education. (2011). *The Handbook for Campus Safety and Security Reporting.* Retrieved from: http://www.ed.gov/admins/lead/safety/campus.html.

Ward, D. & Mann, J. L. (2011). *The Handbook for Campus Safety and Security Reporting.* US Department of Education. Retrieved from: http://www2.ed.gov/admins/lead/safety/handbook.pdf.

White House. (2015). *Address to the Nation by the President.* Washington, DC: Office of the Press Secretary. Retrieved from: https://www.whitehouse.gov/the-press-office/2015/12/06/address-nation-president.

CONCLUSION

From the earliest days of the community college, leaders have been faced with the task of managing a variety of challenging issues. As the colleges developed and missions became more comprehensive, the issues changed and became more complex. As we look to the future of the community college and the challenges and opportunities ahead, we believe its leaders will be managing different types of institutions: the most diverse, complex, and exciting generation of institutions in the history of the American community college. The colleges will encounter more change at a faster pace than in any previous generation, and this change and pace will be driven in part by both advances in technology and calls for accountability—and the environment will be more engaging and constituent-centered than many of us dare to imagine today.

Reform and Redesign

In 2015, researchers from the Community College Research Center (CCRC) released a new book, *Redesigning America's Community Colleges: A Clearer Path to Student Success*, that advanced a compelling argument for community colleges to rethink the ways in which they organize academic programs of study and support services. The book examined many current community college reform efforts. CCRC Director Tom Bailey, Assistant Director Shanna Smith Jaggars, and Senior Research Associate Davis Jenkins wrote, "We argue that these reforms have not produced the desired outcomes because they have stopped short of making the systemic changes necessary to shift colleges' organizational cultures from a focus on access alone to a focus on access with success" (Bailey, Smith Jaggars, & Jenkins, 2015, p. 3).

According to these researchers, a redesigned community college offers coherent programs of studies that reform the entire student experience from entry to completion. The redesign of community colleges called for by Bailey and his colleagues also requires fundamental changes in the way leaders manage issues and conduct the business of the college. The open-door mission has historically served as the backbone of the community college's prominence in higher education. Even with the challenges and limitations of the open-door mission, community colleges provided access and educational opportunities for millions of Americans on an annual basis—people who might not otherwise have been able to go to college. How many new ideas and new perspectives will truly *redesigned* community colleges produce and how much more quickly will the impact of these changes be felt by community college stakeholders? The success of more students is good both for the individual student and for the communities served by community colleges.

It is likely that reform and redesign of community colleges in one aspect or another will be a continuing process. Managing a wide range of issues will be a part of every community college leader's professional life, and some may struggle to describe what leadership was like before the eras of increased accountability and attention to college completion rates. As calls for increased accountability, completion, and success force more community colleges to change or redesign, we remind community college stakeholders that managing issues is intricately intertwined with every redesign and change initiative. Attempts to increase student success rates while maintaining access and increasing quality will be a continuing challenge at all levels. Local community colleges, along with the state and national organizations that represent them, will all address the emerging issues and challenges to ensure that community colleges remain at the forefront of advancing higher education opportunity and success.

Accountability and Transparency

We believe that local communities and the country as a whole will be the net beneficiaries of effective community colleges, experiencing the positive impact of educated citizens and a well-trained workforce. But despite the almost universally recognized benefits of community colleges, leaders will still be faced with the issues of calls for increased levels of accountability and transparency. Community college leaders will be expected to demonstrate through verifiable results how responsive they are to internal and external stakeholders and whether outcomes meet expectations. Contemporary accountability efforts like those articulated in chapter 3 indicate that community colleges are undergoing major transformation in terms of what it means to be accountable and transparent.

Change and the Evolving Mission

So, what do we know about the next generation of community colleges? First, it is clear that access is not the only mission focus for community colleges, yet access is still critical to the mission of community colleges. We discussed how the community college's open-door policies provide access to, and opportunity for, education through programs and services that respond to community needs and provide education and life-changing credentials for individuals. We highlighted some of the mission-related issues that community college leaders will have to navigate as they focus on maintaining the open door and respond to student needs while managing both internal and external policies and mandates. In the future, community colleges will couple access with student success and completion to assist students to enter the college and to attain their goals. Community college leaders will increasingly use data to help them make key decisions that affect the viability of their institutions. College leaders will also use technology to run predictive analytics from data warehouses to assist in attracting, retaining, and graduating students. Although colleges will use technology to support them, leaders will still need the skills to make informed decisions and to assign responsibility to appropriate team members to execute the decisions.

Diversity, Equity, and Inclusion

Issues of diversity, equity, and inclusion will affect how the colleges conduct their business and interact with stakeholders. The increasingly diverse student populations at community colleges have presented new and different leadership challenges for community college educators. Diversity, equity, and inclusion issues will continue to emerge inside and outside the classroom. Community college leaders must be knowledgeable of these issues and be prepared to make the decisions that are necessary to enhance learning outcomes for underrepresented students and to improve faculty engagement.

Stakeholder Demands

Contemporary and future community college leaders will be expected to manage institutions in the midst of growing demands from internal and external stakeholders, increased governmental policies and mandates, interest from the media, and shifting relationships with business communities that look to community colleges for the training of skilled workers. A variety of groups have a stake in the business of any community college. Stakeholders can generate governance and public relations problems that are not always easy for community college leaders to solve. However, community college leaders must strive to support governance systems that ensure stakeholders have appropriate opportunities to inform decision making at the institution. A community college leader's ability to manage governance issues in a collaborative manner is essential for the current and future welfare of the institution. The ability to manage the media, including social media, has become an essential skill for any leader.

Safety and Security

Finally, college leaders need to lead efforts to improve campus safety and security management and define a new set of issues dealing with the privacy of both students and employees. Community colleges will need to create new policies and procedures to ensure that precautions are being taken to provide a safe and secure campus and to take appropriate actions to guard against cybersecurity threats. Safety and security issue management will require institutions to collect and store more personal information about stakeholders than ever before—and to do it in ways that protect the security of data. An important aspect of managing safety and security concerns is the extent to which the leader can encourage students, employees, and campus visitors to join in creating and maintaining a safe and secure educational campus environment. Athletic coaches must take appropriate actions to ensure that player safety is their first priority. The leader will also need to understand the importance of an up-to-date emergency preparedness plan and of filing annual security reports detailing college policies and crime statistics as required by federal law.

New Requirements for Leadership

What emerges for community colleges now and in the future is a tale of two leadership cultures. One is the present that has developed over multiple generations of community colleges—and the other is still being shaped by emerging internal and external issues. Though historical practices may sometimes delay the development of new ones, relying on old ways of managing will make it harder for leaders to address contemporary issues. In our view, managing issues in community colleges requires egalitarian and transparent practices that can make leadership more interesting, relevant, and effective.

Rewards of Leadership

The challenges that today's leaders face may seem daunting to some readers. But it is not our intent to discourage capable individuals from seeking leadership roles in the nation's community colleges. On the contrary, both of us view our time as college leaders as the highlight of our careers in education. In fact, the rewards of college leadership are significant. In no other position can an educator have the opportunity to lead the transformation of an institution for the betterment of all stakeholders. Although presidents are the most easily identified college leaders, leadership is not restricted to them. Appropriate and effective leadership is needed at all levels of an institution, including governing boards, foundation boards, advisory groups, administrators, faculty, staff, and students. We wrote this book to assist these leaders as they work to make our world a better place.

REFERENCE

Bailey, T. R., Jaggars, S. S., & Jenkins, D. (2015). *Redesigning America's Community Colleges: A Clearer Path to Student Success*. Cambridge, MA: Harvard University Press.

INDEX

K

Katzenbach, Jon, 144
Kingsborough Community
College learning community
program, 35
Kirkwood Community College
data breach, 175
Kotter, J. P., 141, 153–154

L

Leaders: AACC on competencies
of, 2; incivility attacks, 132; life
balance for, 10
Leadership: AACC on
advocacy of, 73; contingency
theory on, 1; curricula
development programs, 2;
issues management, 1–12;
multidimensional perspective
of, 2; new requirements for,
184; rewards of, 184–185;
safety and security commitment,
167; transactional and
transformational theories on, 1
League for Innovation in
the Community College,
*Democracy's Colleges: Call to
Action* statement, 22
Learning analytics, for student
support, 149
*A Learning College for the 21st
Century* (O'Banion), 19
Learning College generation, from
1990 to 2000, 19, 20
Learning college movement, 20
Learning community
programs, 35, 147
Learning environment, for African
Americans, 86

Learning Paradigm, 142
"The Learning Paradigm"
(Boggs), 19
Learning styles, 85
Legal implications review, in issues
management model, 9
Legislative mandates:
developmental education
courses, 26; high school
enrichment programs, 25–26;
remedial education, 25–26;
standardized tests use, 25
Lesbian, gay, bisexual, and
transgender (LGBT) issues, DEI
and, 95–96
Levine, John, 16–17
Lewin, Kurt, 141
LGBT. *See* Lesbian, gay, bisexual,
and transgender
Life balance, 10
Local higher education authority,
in media relations strategy, 121
Lone Star College System
pre-collegiate program,
23–24
Lumina Foundation, 31,
34, 35, 51

M

*MAE. See Military
Advanced Education*
Maricopa Community College
District: *31 Days of Cyber
Security Tips*, 175–176; data
breach, 175
MCC. *See* Metropolitan
Community College
McClenney, Byron, 2
MCHSs. *See* Middle College
High Schools